‖‖‖ ‖‖‖‖‖‖‖‖‖‖‖‖‖‖‖‖‖‖‖‖
⟨✓ **W9-CEJ-162**

"I am privileged to be able to endorse a book that deals so well with my passion; that is, helping God's people handle God's money. David and Debbie are extremely well qualified to offer practical and encouraging advice in this area. I enthusiastically recommend this book to those interested in getting their financial house in order."

Ron Blue
Ron Blue & Co., LLC

"Dave and Debbie creatively use the word picture of building a house to make God's financial principles come alive. The master bedroom humorously describes the unique money-handling differences between men and women and gives practical tools for understanding each other and opening up lines of communication. Those who apply the principles in this book will discover God's true blessings and have a floorplan for getting their financial house in order."

Gary Smalley
Smalley Relationship Center

"Every couple we've ever encountered—no matter how much they make—has money squabbles. It is the number-one source of conflict in marriage. Period. Whether you are newlyweds or seasoned veterans, Dave and Debbie Bragonier offer expert guidance for helping you balance your love ledger as well as your books. Immensely practical and biblically sound, *Getting Your Financial House in Order* is for every married couple."

Drs. Les and Leslie Parrott, Seattle Pacific University
Authors, *When Bad Things Happen to Good Marriages*

"We have had many couples come into our lives in the forty-eight-plus years we have been married, and financial problems are a common complaint. In this book, Dave and Debbie give you some very practical tools to help with building, repairing, and maintaining your financial house. Included is a room-by-room tour of what a successful financial house looks like and a way to determine the health of your present financial house. Dave and Debbie are flexible and recognize the need to accept differences in people. . . . The Bragoniers remind us that it's not the amount of money we have that's important; it's our *attitude* toward the money that counts. We highly recommend this practical blueprint to *Getting Your Financial House in Order.*"

Chuck and Barb Snyder
World's Most Opposite Couple

"Are you ready for a hammer-and-nails, biblically based, easy, fun-to-read guide to God's plan for you and your resources? Here it is!"

Norm and Bobbe Evans
Pro Athletes Outreach

Portage Public Library
2665 Irving Street
Portage, IN 46368

"Want to get your financial house in order? Need help in teaching your children financial skills? Help is available from a couple who has spent most of their married life in developing, teaching, and modeling God's principles for handling money. I highly recommend the Bragoniers' *Getting Your Financial House in Order*. Their book provides information and instruction helpful to all ages and all income levels."

Charles L. Collings,
CEO Emeritus, Raley's

"I have known the Bragoniers for more than ten years, and they have on a number of occasions helped teach our congregation God's principles for money management. Their new book contains remarkably practical insights for building and maintaining your financial house. They have made effective use of construction metaphors to arm you with new skills and perspectives to bring order and purpose to an area that you may find an overwhelming challenge. We live in an overly consumptive culture, and this book is a must read for those who desire to please God with their finances."

Gary Gulbranson, Senior Pastor
Westminster Chapel, Bellevue, Washington

"David and Debbie Bragonier give readers a toolkit to get their financial house in order. This book puts financial principles in easy-to-understand terms. Chapters are designed around various rooms in a house. Their step-by-step walk through the house helps readers review their financial status and make necessary changes, supplying outstanding Scripture references for the basic principles. After completing this book the readers should have developed or revised a financial floorplan that will give them a new freedom and a closer walk with Christ. . . .

"David and Debbie use biblical principles to show the real key to financial freedom is not how much money you have, but how you apply God's principles to your finances—'knowing exactly where God wants you and pressing forward in the areas you need to improve.'

"By applying these principles the readers will experience true financial freedom and improve their walk with Christ."

Bob Williams, President
Evergreen Freedom Foundation

"During our days of playing football and hosting player couples in our home for growing successful lives, Dave and Debbie were trusted and enlightening guides to timeless and practical financial stewardship. The valuable game plan in this book is especially needed today as we aim to restore the strength of marriages and families that are frequently derailed by financial ignorance and confusion."

Jeff Kemp, Executive Director
Families Northwest

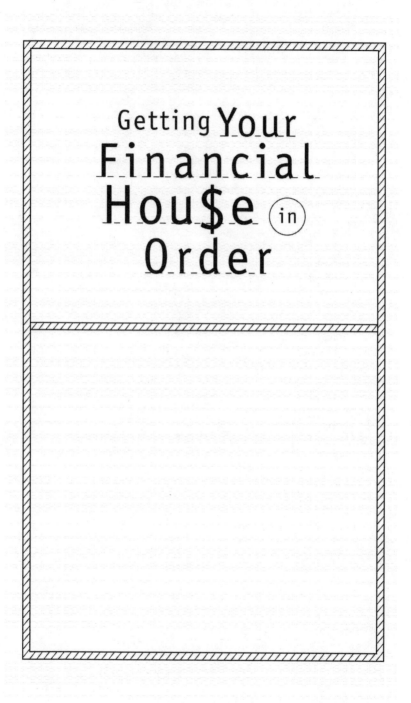

Getting Your Financial Hou$e in Order

Getting Your Financial Hou$e (in) Order

A Floorplan for Managing Your Money

David AND Debbie Bragonier

WITH **K.S. Gollnick**

PORTER COUNTY PUBLIC LIBRARY SYSTEM

Portage Public Library
2665 Irving Street
Portage, IN 46368

APR 1 3 2004

BROADMAN
&HOLMAN
PUBLISHERS

Nashville, Tennessee

332.024 BRA   POR
Bragonier, David
Getting your financial
house in order : a
33410007381603

© 2003 by David and Debbie Bragonier
All rights reserved.
Printed in the United States of America

0-8054-2720-1

Published by Broadman & Holman Publishers
Nashville, Tennessee

Dewey Decimal Classification: 332.024
Subject Heading: PERSONAL FINANCE \ HOUSEHOLD BUDGET

Unless otherwise stated all Scripture citation is from the Holy Bible,
New International Version, © 1973, 1978, 1984 by International
Bible Society. Other versions cited are the HCSB, Holman Christian
Standard Bible®, © 1999, 2000, 2002, by Holman Bible Publishers,
and NASB, the New American Standard Bible, © the Lockman
Foundation, 1960, 1962, 1963, 1968, 1971, 1972, 1973, 1975, 1977,
used by permission.

1 2 3 4 5 6 7 8 9 10 07 06 05 04 03

DEDICATIONS

For years we heard the persistent prodding, "publish or perish," from our close friends George and Liz Toles. We are grateful for them helping us launch the ideas for this book. We thank them for their investment in our lives, marriage, family, and work. We wholeheartedly dedicate this book to them.

—David and Debbie Bragonier

For my parents, who first taught me God's principles on money.

—KG

ACKNOWLEDGMENTS

We wish to thank our parents, Bill and Jeanette Bragonier and Marge Venema, for their examples and wise financial management. Their years of faithful support and unconditional love created a framework for us to observe, learn from, and apply in our lives.

We thank our children, Julie, Christy, John, Michael, and Matthew for providing all the wonderful, funny, and real-life illustrations for our seminars and for this book (especially Julie and Christy). If we missed any that are funny or embarrassing, don't fret—we'll do our best to expose you in future publications.

We appreciate the Barnabas Board of Directors for believing in us and giving years of support.

We wish to thank Kimn Gollnick for her dedication and persistence. She helped us sound brilliant with her talented writing and did everything possible to adapt our style and convey the message from our hearts to you.

In this entire process we have seen God's hand at work. Thanks to all who helped make this dream come true. We are eternally grateful. We recognize that everything we are or have comes from God and others who have contributed to our lives.

Blessings,
David and Debbie Bragonier

CONTENTS

FOREWORD

I came to know David before Crown Ministries and Christian Financial Concepts merged to form Crown Financial Ministries. I had heard about Dave's heart, ministry, and seminars from friends like George Fooshee, a financial author and Crown board member.

One of our ministry's core values is a commitment to developing relationships. I do not know any seminar teacher more gifted at instantly developing a relationship with an audience than Dave Bragonier. You will feel this same personal connection as you read *Getting Your Financial House in Order*. His wife Debbie also shares her perspective, experiences, and insights in this outstanding book.

This gifted couple has helped tens of thousands of people get their financial houses in biblical order. Take an exciting, life-changing walk with them as they share their hearts, their experiences, and God's Word. Applying these principles will enable you to experience real financial freedom and grow closer to our Lord and Savior Jesus Christ. May God bless you as you learn from this choice couple God's financial principles.

Howard Dayton
CEO
Crown Financial Ministries

INTRODUCTION

By wisdom a house is built,
    and through understanding it is established;
through knowledge its rooms are filled
    with rare and beautiful treasures.
                —PROVERBS 24:3-4

O ur guess is that you probably have this book in your hand because you desire to get your finances in better order. Whether you're just starting out or you're an old pro— whether the repair work needed is minor or major—we each need help, education, encouragement, and accountability for handling money.

We appreciate your willingness to get your financial house in order. Your actions will benefit many—you, your spouse and family (or future spouse and family), and your community.

Keep your attention focused on the principles you learn in this book. It's easy to admire friends who appear to have their act together and who freely buy what they want. The media paints the same picture: You can have it all! However, statistics prove otherwise. The truth is that many people look good on the outside and seem to have financial freedom, but behind closed doors their world is in shambles. In our many years of financial counseling, we've seen this personally—people with lives full of stress, finances out of control, marriages hanging by a thread, and children steeped in rebellion.

There are many opportunities and pressures bidding for your valuable time. However, nothing impacts your life more than your daily walk with God and your management of money and its related matters. God will bless you as you open your life

1

to Him and His biblical principles, moving forward one day at a time.

We'd like to pray for you.

Father in heaven, we give you thanks for all you've given to us. We know You love us. We know You want your best for all areas of our lives, including finances. We know You don't really care where we've been; You only care where we're going. Your Son Jesus Christ paid the price for everything in our past. We now ask for Your wisdom, discernment, and understanding regarding the finances You've entrusted to us. Lord, clear away the clutter from our lives and the things that would distract us from getting our finances in order. Help us to focus on what You have for us. Give us the strength to apply each of the principles in Your Word to our lives and finances. May we and the resources You entrust to us be mighty tools in Your hand, used for Your glory and Your purposes. We ask this in the name of Jesus Christ. Amen.

Your Financial House

Our word picture for this book is one of building, repairing, and maintaining a financial house. In the following chapters, we will walk through different rooms of our financial house, examining the floor plan from a biblical perspective on finance.

What do you wish your financial house looked like? Clean, uncluttered, easy to walk from room to room without worry or concern? Together, we will address each of these issues.

We will also introduce you to our financial toolbox. To build or repair a house takes tools. It also requires safety instructions and in many cases, some ground work.

As you walk through the chapters and your "house," you will notice that each room represents a different aspect of your finances. Understand, this analogy is not in Scripture, but the financial principles are. Many of the rooms we chose make sense and have a certain parallel to personal finances.

For instance, after we sit on the front porch and examine the blueprints (our past financial mistakes and future possibilities), we'll walk into the entryway, where we ponder the architect and design (whose house is it?). The living room is for realistic goal setting and planning. The kitchen is where we blend financial ingredients together to make things work on a daily basis. Here's where we will address budgeting, the recipe for financial freedom. Or, if you don't like the word *budgeting*, you can use *planning* or *cash-flow management system.*

We will also visit the master bedroom. Because men and women see money from two different perspectives, they wonder why things get so heated between them when the topic of money comes up. The principles and applications in this room are a key to financial success as it relates to husbands and wives.

Other rooms we'll tour include the dining room, the place where we practice hospitality (giving and charities). The den is where we take care of long-term financial matters such as insurance, investing, wills, savings, and retirement. The children's room covers children's attitudes about money, allowances, gifts, etc.

One of the most important rooms in this financial house model addresses the subject of debt, credit cards, mortgages, and many other life-impacting financial decisions. As we considered which room best represents this part of our finances (debt and other negative aspects), we first thought of the bathroom—flushing away bad, negative habits. However, it didn't seem like the best word picture. Fortunately, it took Debbie only a second to suggest the laundry room, a place where we wash away dirt from our clothes, and in a sense, our lives (bad habits and overuse of credit).

Near the end of our tour, we will gather in the guest room, where we'll discuss additional tips for single parents. In the final chapter, we'll head over to the garage to discuss the repair and maintenance of our finances and our financial plans.

Throughout this book, in each "room" you will find scriptural principles, practical applications, real-life illustrations, and a challenge to you, to write out needed steps of action.

If you will walk through the rooms of your financial house and honestly address the issues that become apparent, we guarantee that God will start to do a mighty work in your life. He will reduce financial stress, increase the peace you have in your life, and start you on the path to His "true" financial freedom. Come, let's get started getting your financial house in order.

CHAPTER 1

The Front Porch

Reflecting on the Past, Seeing a Vision for the Future

Many, O LORD my God,
    are the wonders you have done.
The things you planned for us
    no one can recount to you;
were I to speak and tell of them,
    they would be too many to declare.
                    —PSALM 40:5

C ome sit on the front porch for a few minutes. Let's do some reflecting and dreaming. Reflecting can be a little painful, but the dreaming is fun.

What does your current financial house look like? Is it simply in need of minor repairs, or does it need a major remodel? Do you control your finances, or do you feel as if your finances control you?

	Yes	No
Do you feel free from stress when bills are due?	—	—
Are you free from worrying about money?	—	—
Do you have a plan, including written goals and a written budget?	—	—

	Yes	No
Do you follow your written plan (your budget)?	—	—
Do you balance your checking account(s) to the penny each month?	—	—
Are you setting aside money for car repairs, house maintenance, gifts, etc.?	—	—
Do you pay cash for automobiles?	—	—
Do you pay your bills and credit companies on time?	—	—
Do you pay off your credit card balance each month?	—	—
Do you limit credit cards to one or two?	—	—
Are you currently paying extra to accelerate payoff of your mortgage?	—	—
Do you give to charities each month (or annually)?	—	—
Are you satisfied with your amount of charitable giving?	—	—
Do you give away a percentage of your income each year?	—	—
In the past year, have you helped someone financially in his/her time of need?	—	—
Do you have adequate insurance (health, life, disability, auto, house)?	—	—
Do you have short-term savings for emergencies?	—	—
Do you participate in your employer's retirement plan?	—	—
If not, do you have your own retirement plan?	—	—
Do you have a current will or trust?	—	—
Do you regularly teach your children about money management?	—	—
In the past month have you discussed money management with them?	—	—
Total each column:	—	—

If you had ten or more no answers, your financial house needs help—quick! You've taken the first step by reading this book. Be ready to dig deep and work on building or remodeling your financial house and getting it in order.

If you had ten or more yes answers, your financial house is probably in good shape but may need a little decluttering or perhaps an update (remodeling). Use this book to help you isolate areas that need attention. Look for blind spots or zones where improvement is needed, such as described in chapter 5, "Master Bedroom: Husband and Wife Financial Communication." Continue reviewing your budget and financial plans regularly. Review your goals. Is there more you could accomplish?

You may be aware that some of these answers indicate symptoms of financial bondage. We understand. Before we started seriously addressing our own finances, we felt stress and defeat in many of these same areas.

What did our financial house look like before we started applying God's principles and budgeting our money?

Before we share our story, we'd like to set some guidelines for the personal illustrations we share in this book.

Guideline 1—God has a plan for you and your finances, which may differ from His plan for us in our finances. Certainly, we should all rely on the plumb line of the Bible, holding up God's principles to keep each of us in check scripturally. However, He is not going to tell me the specific plan He has for you. In reading our stories, you may see God working in our lives in certain matters that may not be His specific plan for you. This leads to the next guideline.

Guideline 2—What is a freedom for me may not be a freedom for you. What is a freedom for you may not be a freedom for me—and both can be in God's will. God works His perfect will in each of our lives differently (Rom. 14:2–8).

Guideline 3—We have not arrived. We work at these principles and practical applications every day of our married life together. The key is how fast we acknowledge reality, seek and find the truth, and correct the mistake. Even then, God may or may not choose to eliminate or lessen the consequences of our actions. If He does, we smile at His love and mercy.

Guideline 4—There are spiritual principles of money management that apply to everyone. That's why we call the Bible our plumb line. Our goal in this book is to help you see those plumb line principles and then apply them.

Caution: If you tie success to monetary wealth, you probably have the wrong couple in mind for role models. By a global standard, we are financially wealthy since most of the world lives in complete poverty. However, by the average American's concept of wealth, we would not qualify. We are not millionaires or even close.

However, one day we acknowledged our irresponsibility and started applying God's financial principles. Shortly after that we stepped out in faith in full-time ministry work. At that time, we wondered how we would pay our bills, save for car repairs, fund Christmas, or save toward retirement—all the same concerns most people struggle over.

PLUMB LINE PRINCIPLE
And my God will supply all your needs according to His riches in glory in Christ Jesus.
—Philippians 4:19 HCSB

Well, since that time, God has given us His peace as we applied biblical principles to our financial decisions. He funded our needs. We have never used consumer debt or financed a car in all those years. We are also saving yearly toward retirement. We have the peace that surpasses all understanding. He will do the same for you.

We'd like to give you a snapshot of where we were financially when we started our journey. We had a nice house and the mortgage to go with it. Dave had a company car, so our secondary car didn't need to be expensive, and we didn't like to borrow money for cars. However, we weren't budgeting our money, and we were having serious husband-and-wife money talks. We had also overextended our buying, using the credit cards we carried. We could not save any money, and we didn't have a retirement plan.

How did we start getting our financial house in order? The same way the majority of couples do—through the promptings and encouragement of the wife.

For years, Debbie said, "Dave, we need to get on a budget." I would flippantly respond, "We don't have the money to go on a budget. Go to the grocery store and don't spend a lot of money."

So off she reluctantly went to the grocery store, worrying about how much she should spend. Of course, I would be at home worrying about how much she would spend. One day it dawned on me (again, probably through her promptings) that we were spending a certain amount of money at the grocery store anyway, so why not figure out how much it is and how it fits into our income and other expenses?

That was the beginning of our path to financial freedom. As we indicated earlier, none of us "arrives" when it comes to financial management. Just about the time you think you have it all figured out, God may allow a new financial challenge into your life to see how you are doing in the area of faith and trust in Him.

But you can have peace if you follow His principles.

Understand, financial freedom is not related to the amount of money you have. You can have millions of dollars in the bank and still be in financial bondage. Financial bondage comes in all shapes, sizes, and colors.

Can you detect which of these people are in bondage?

Example 1: This person makes $40,000 a year, has about $22,000 in credit card debt and can't pay her creditors on time. She is driving a car she really can't afford, and her house payment is too big for her income. She can't save any money, and she worries all the time.

Example 2: With this married couple, both husband and wife work outside the home. They have a good income; they have no major debt or credit card problems. However, they feel they can't survive without her income, yet they want children and are aware of the potential benefits of having a stay-at-home parent. They save very little money and feel they barely keep their heads above water. They feel trapped by their circumstances.

Example 3: This married couple makes more than $75,000 a year. They have no debt, and they pay all their monthly obligations on time. They save money, have investments, and always live within their means. They take nice vacations and can basically buy most anything they want within reason. However, they tend to argue about money and expenditures, both large and small. The husband or wife comments to the other, "You're spending too much." They frequently worry about not having enough for the future. They prepare an annual budget, but if they underspend for the year, they don't feel any freedom to carry the leftover amounts into next year's budget categories or to use some of the excess funds to buy something they want.

Example 4: This person has $5 million in liquid assets. He has no debt and is very concerned about his investments. He takes excessive time to manage his affairs and is known by friends as the man who always buys the two-day-old doughnuts, never buying any fresh ones. He doesn't believe in contributing any of his wealth to charities.

OK, which of these examples reveals a person or couple who is in bondage? We're sure you guessed correctly—all of them are in financial bondage. It's not the amount of money you have that's important; it's your *attitude* about the money that counts. That is why we're thankful you're reading this book. Our goal is to help you get your financial house in order, to set you free from financial bondage, and thereby help you become completely available for fruitful service to God.

Press Forward

Remember, God doesn't care where you've been, just where you're going. Don't be hard on yourself if you saw yourself identified in the above examples. Keep your eyes focused on what's ahead of you, not what's in the past or behind you.

Even when you physically build a house (which we have done), you will find there are always things you would have done a little differently. Most of those things can be fixed or adjusted later. The key for your financial situation is to work on the big picture first, then on the details later.

> Not that I have already reached the goal or am
> already fully mature, but I make every effort . . .
> forgetting what is behind and reaching forward
> to what is ahead,

I pursue as my goal the prize promised by God's
heavenly call in Christ Jesus.
—Philippians 3:12–14 HCSB

Goals

Allow us to give you an overview of our goals for this book:

1. To encourage you to study what the Bible says regarding financial principles.
2. To start you on the road to God's true financial freedom. Most people have a wrong concept of financial freedom and therefore they are not free. Remember, financial freedom doesn't have to do with how much money you have; it has to do with applying God's principles, knowing you are exactly where God wants you, and pressing forward in the areas you need to improve.
3. To help you discover and fulfill your personal financial goals. What does God want you to accomplish? Remember, God has a plan for your life, and He's not going to tell us what that plan is. This book is just the starting point. You may need input and help from other professionals as you walk down the road to financial freedom.
4. To help strengthen marriages and families. We personally believe that from the beginning of time, the enemy (Satan) has been trying to destroy the godly seed, a part of which is the family structure. Satan failed at the cross and the resurrection of Jesus Christ, so now he's after you and me. He wants to destroy the family and the remnant of Christians, thereby claiming victory here on earth.

Satan wants us to live a life of mediocrity—financial and otherwise. Most people don't realize that he has them targeted for bondage. He doesn't usually knock on the front door and say, "Here I am." Instead, he's stealthy. He slides in the back door and ties us up financially—sometimes slowly, over time, thereby making us unavailable for God's work. This can happen simply through ignorance; we don't know or understand (God's) financial principles because no one taught us.

When we are bound financially, it restricts us from true worship of God. It takes us out of service to His work. While at church, we may find ourselves thinking and worrying about next week and our problems. Financial pressures and related time commitments keep us from serving as we would like to serve.

God has a unique calling for you. He wants to do a mighty work in your life. In Jeremiah 29:11–13 we read, "'For I know the plans I have for you,' declares the Lord, 'plans to prosper you and not to harm you, plans to give you hope and a future. Then you will call upon me and come and pray to me, and I will listen to you. You will seek me and find me when you seek me with all your heart.'"

Our hope is that you will seek God's will with all your heart and follow His principles—not only in finances but in your spiritual walk, as well.

A Vision for Your Financial House

God is not a God of disorder but of peace.
—1 Corinthians 14:33a HCSB

Well, we've been sitting on the front porch. You've been thinking about your current condition. How you feel right now will depend on your personal situation. You may be feeling there is no hope. Or you may be thinking, *This is great; I'm well on my way.* If you're feeling the former, don't despair. Remember, it doesn't matter where you've been—only where you're going. You simply need to walk forward one step at a time, one day at a time.

You are now aware of certain problems, perhaps even chaos, in your financial house. Let's think about where you would like to be and what you want your financial house to look like in the future (both near and distant).

God is a God of order. Our guess is that most people don't want chaos. Most people want things to be in some kind of order. We want to know that we have enough money for today's expenses and can prepare for future needs.

Where are you headed? Are you simply walking aimlessly through life, working where you don't want to work? Are you feeling hopeless and depressed? Remember, God wants to do a mighty work in your life. We simply need to cooperate, do the appropriate planning, and keep moving forward in the process. Ask yourself this question: "What would I like to accomplish in my lifetime?"

PLUMB LINE PRINCIPLE
Delight yourself in the Lord and he will give you the desires of your heart.
—Psalm 37:4

A few years ago we were at a radio station preparing to tape programs. One of our guests asked us an eye-opening question: "If you didn't have to earn any more money, what would you spend your time doing?"

Wow! What a soul-searching question. Some people might instantly respond, "Play golf every day." How would you answer that question?

The question is, if you didn't have to earn a living, what would you spend your time doing? Most likely, our answer will differ from yours in specific details. However, we hope it would be similar at heart—like spending more time in ministry, helping others.

What would you do, and how would you spend your time if you didn't have to earn any more money?

Take time right now to jot down your answer to this question. In the coming chapters, take time to complete the Goals Worksheet included in the back of this book. Be very specific. Include details.

Ultimately, your honest, personal answers may help you set up the rest of your financial house plans and help prioritize which rooms need your attention first.

CHAPTER 2

Tools of the Trade, Safety Instructions, and Leveling the Ground

Teach me to do your will,
for you are my God;
may your good Spirit
lead me on level ground.
—PSALM 143:10

The Financial Toolbox

To work on your financial house, you need a financial toolbox. Let's look at some of the tools you may need:

Plumb Line

We learned when we built our house that it's absolutely crucial to have the foundation and framing very straight and aligned perfectly.

The only financial plumb line that will always be accurate, correct, and true is the Bible. The Bible gives very clear directions on not only how to live our lives but also how to handle money. Popular wisdom in the culture, and even at times the well-meaning advice from our Christian friends, may be 180 degrees opposite of what God's Word instructs. We live in a society that uses the TV, radio, or computer at all hours. We're bombarded from many sides with ideas, philosophies, propaganda, and financial get-rich-quick schemes. If we listen to these sources long enough, we're susceptible to their messages, including their wrong agendas. We need the Word of God as the plumb line to guide us.

PLUMB LINE PRINCIPLE

Blessed is the man who makes the Lord his trust, who does not look to the proud, to those who turn aside to false gods.
—*Psalm 40:4*

Tape Measure

We use this to measure distances. Our financial tape measure helps us determine our immediate needs and distant goals. What's the distance from today to the point when we can check off an action item as completed or fulfilled? The Bible also tells us to carefully "count the cost" (Luke 14:28–30). What will it take to get you from your current situation to financial freedom? "The carpenter measures with a line and makes an outline with a marker; . . . I have made you, you are my servant; . . . Return to me, for I have redeemed you" (Isa. 44:13a, 21–22b).

Crowbar

You may need a crowbar to knock down walls or remove barriers. Maybe you have some longtime habits, perhaps even unacknowledged at this point, that will have to be addressed. There may be areas of your life that you may not even realize are contrary to God's Word. We must knock down these walls if we're going to construct a financial house that's plumb with God's Word. "I will take away its hedge, and it will be destroyed; I will break down its wall, and it will be trampled" (Isa. 5:5b).

Saw

You will need a saw to cut things out or cut them to size, in order to make everything fit properly. You might know, or will soon discover, that your expenses do not fit your income. Therefore, you must cut some expenses. You may need to cut or redesign priorities to accomplish the important instead of only the urgent. Some may need to reshape careers or revenue sources to increase income or gross profits. Before you start hacking away, however, keep in mind you can be creative in the process. Always measure twice before every cut. Don't do anything drastic at this point. We will address this more fully in chapter 7, "Kitchen: A Recipe for Financial Freedom (Planning and Budgeting)."

Hammer

A hammer is used for driving nails or stakes. Nails and stakes hold things firm. In financial disciplines we need to stand in the trenches and say, "I'm making a stand for this cause or goal. I'm driving a stake on the biblical principle, not on what others say regarding this issue." We will point out biblical standards throughout this book.

Other Tools

We need pliers and vice grips to grab and hold concepts or new ideas. Screwdrivers help us tighten things up a little, or do some fine-tuning. Time or pressure has loosened some small financial disciplines we know or used to practice. These disciplines may need adjusting and tightening in your financial house.

Needle-nose pliers, wire cutters, plastic tape, and other such items are used for making electrical repairs and mending damaged wires or communication devices. You may need to mend wounded relationships and broken lines of communication. This repair work is very valid in the marriage relationship. You and your spouse may both carry spoken and unspoken financial hurts and frustrations. This surfaces all the time in our seminars and previous counseling ministry. There can be unmet expectations or spousal responsibilities. Such issues need to be identified and repaired. We will give you specific instruction and helps in chapter 5, "Master Bedroom."

Level

A level is a very important tool. All of us must find balance in our daily lives, marriages, careers, child rearing, hobbies, and recreation. It's best to avoid extremes. Personally, we know we can get out of balance. That's why we're thankful God gave us each other, as husband and wife. There are times when all of us need help keeping a proper balance in our lives and finances. Accountability is covered later in this chapter, under "Safety Instructions."

Stud Finder

For the ladies, this is not a Christian matchmaker! This tool helps you find wall studs behind the drywall where the framing boards are located, so you can mark them for strong support when hanging shelves or cabinets. We need a stud finder to help us see behind the obvious so we hang our financial framework on solid supports. The Holy Spirit plays an important part in our commitment to follow God's financial principles. "'Not by might nor by power, but by my Spirit,' says the LORD Almighty" (Zech. 4:6). "The Spirit also joins to help in our weakness, because we do not know what to pray for as we should, but the Spirit Himself intercedes for us. . . . And He who searches the hearts knows the Spirit's mind-set, because He intercedes for the saints according to the will of God" (Rom. 8:26–27 HCSB).

Power Tools

Power tools get the job done faster and make life a lot easier. You will soon recognize when you need professional advisers who can help you with your finances, budgeting, insurance needs, investments, estate planning, etc. These advisers are valuable for their experience. You don't have to reinvent the wheel, and you don't have to be the expert in every financial arena. Besides this book, you may discover you need others—the power tools—to make building or remodeling your financial house easier and more successful. "Plans fail for lack of counsel, but with many advisers they succeed" (Prov. 15:22).

Extension Cords

Extension cords are important. Extension cords help us reach beyond our limitations. In the area of finances, we— not God or other people—usually set most of our limitations ourselves. "In all these things we are more than victorious through Him who loved us" (Rom. 8:37 HCSB).

Plunger or Snake

These are invaluable for unclogging drains. Maybe you have drains that are clogged in your life or in your finances, or maybe you're caught in a rut. You may need to clean out those areas in order to move forward. "A man's own folly ruins his life" (Prov. 19:3). "If you, O LORD, kept a record of sins, O LORD, who could stand? But with you there is forgiveness" (Ps. 130:3–4a).

Decorating Tools

Last but not least are tools for painting rooms and hanging wallpaper. These tools provide color and beauty in our homes, enriching our lives. God is the author of beauty. For whatever reason, some people overlook this need for enrichment in their lives. Men in particular tend to miss the importance of those details of enrichment while dealing with the bigger picture or the bottom line. But they are no less important. "He has made everything beautiful in its time" (Eccles. 3:11a).

**PLUMB
LINE
PRINCIPLE**
*The house of the
wicked will be
destroyed, but the
tent of the upright
will flourish.*
—Proverbs 14:11

We're absolutely convinced that God wants to do a mighty work in each of our lives, including our finances, marriage, family, career, and our futures. All we need to do is surrender to God and follow His biblical (financial) principles.

Remember, it does not matter where you've been in the past. It only matters where you're going. Use these biblical tools to help you move forward and make progress.

Safety Instructions and Preparing the Ground (Ground Rules)

We are still on the porch. So far we have spent time reflecting (ouch), dreaming (nothing is impossible), and reviewing the tools in our toolbox (Tim the Tool Man is smiling). If you haven't gone to the back of this book and recorded your thoughts and immediate needs or started an action item list, take time to do that now before you read on.

Then, as with any project, we have some safety instructions and ground rules. We can hear the silent groans from all the male readers. In fact, Tim the Tool Man probably just tossed the book onto the workbench! However, when building a house, both safety instructions and proper preparation of the ground are very important. Women tend to be better at reading instructions than men. Men, please don't overlook the following important points, principles, and practical matters. We know you want to jump in and get started. You're thinking, "If I get into trouble, I'll read the rules later." You can't afford to make that mistake this time around when dealing with money and relationships.

PLUMB LINE PRINCIPLE
The wisdom of the prudent is to give thought to their ways, but the folly of fools is deception.
—*Proverbs 14:8*

Safety Instructions

1. Pray

Our first safety instruction is to make sure we are actually praying about our finances. So many times when we talked with a couple about their situation, we asked, "Are you praying about this?" They gave us a certain look. We often knew what the look meant: "Well, we're mumbling about it a lot. Does that count?"

As human beings, we tend to behave like the Israelites wandering in the desert in the Old Testament. They mumbled a lot about their circumstances, too, instead of stopping and praying. We should stop, get on our knees, and pray specifically about our financial concerns and needs.

In many portions of the psalms written by King David, he simply cries out to God. He tells God about his life and his everyday, very real problems. His prayers seem to say, "Look, God, my life's a mess. My friends just betrayed me. I'm ducking spears every time I look around. Nobody likes me and life is not going well!"

PLUMB LINE PRINCIPLE
Don't worry about anything, but in everything, through prayer and petition . . . let your requests be made known to God.
—Philippians 4:6 HCSB

There is nothing wrong with crying out to God. In fact, the Bible even encourages us to do so: "Cast all your anxiety on him because he cares for you" (1 Pet. 5:7). David said, "In my distress I called upon the LORD, and cried to my God for help; He heard my voice . . . and my cry for help before Him came into His ears" (Ps. 18:6 NASB).

By crying out to God, we admit we are helpless. We relinquish our finances, our plans, and our desires to God so His will can take precedence in our lives.

Your prayer might sound like this: *God, here's where I am right now. My life is a mess. My marriage is struggling. My finances aren't where they should be. My children are being rebellious. Things at work aren't going well. I'm frustrated and tired. Oh, Lord, please help me! I cry out to You because You are the only real means of hope and help.*

However, don't stop there. Continue: *I confess my sins, frailties, mistakes (financial and otherwise), and murmuring. I purpose to follow You more closely. I purpose to get to know You more intimately by reading Your written Word daily. I purpose to start studying and applying Your financial principles as I read and learn about them. Help me use the grace You've already given me to be courageous and boldly face the next twenty-four hours as well as all You have for me in the future.*

Now get specific about your finances or other needs: *Lord, I need to increase my income, cut my expenses, get the car repaired, stop using credit cards, communicate better with my spouse (or whatever the specifics include). I purpose to start fulfilling my responsibilities this day, and I trust You. I need you to help me overcome and solve some of the consequences of my past actions and irresponsibility, and I give you all the glory now and forever. Amen.* If you're married, we encourage you to pray this prayer together, changing the appropriate "I's" to "we."

What are your needs? Write them here as a prayer to the Lord:

_____

_____

_____

_____

_____

_____

_____

As many days as are possible during the week, our family meets first thing in the morning to study God's Word and to get on our knees and pray. We pray about the same concerns as you. *Lord, we need you to stretch our dollars regarding the car we need to replace. Lord, we've saved what we can and we won't use credit. So manifest Yourself regarding this very real need as we go out and search until you lead us to Your car for our family for this next season of life.*

PLUMB LINE PRINCIPLE
God is our refuge and strength, an ever present help in trouble.
—Psalm 46:1

Over the years we have watched God manifest Himself in so many wonderful ways. He has helped us buy cars way beyond the value of the money we saved. It took discipline and it took patience, but the rewards are a part of true financial freedom and true fellowship with Jesus Christ, our intimate and personal Savior.

2. Study God's Word

As mentioned above, another safety instruction is to study God's Word, the Bible. As in sports, we need to study the rule book. In building or remodeling, we need to study the blueprint. This means spending time each day reading and studying the Bible.

Is there a time every day, before you head off to do what you do, that you spend time in God's Word? And for you, men: What is God saying to you and your family this day, regarding your current circumstances, issues, and finances?

If you're married and have a family, are you and your family spending time together in God's Word? This is a priority in our family. As mentioned, when Dave isn't traveling, our family meets first thing in the morning to study God's Word and pray together. When I (Dave) travel, Debbie gathers the family together. I know what they're reading, so I can read the same thing and ask questions of application when I talk with my children on the phone.

PLUMB LINE PRINCIPLE
The statutes of the Lord are trustworthy, making wise the simple. . . . They are more precious than gold.
—*Psalm 19:7b, 10a*

To accomplish our goal of meeting together like this, it means we have to schedule everything around this priority. I (Dave) wake my family early, and we spend time together before I leave for the day. It also means I don't do many breakfast meetings. It's more important that we gather as a family than it is for me to do early morning meetings.

3. Find an Accountability Partner

If you're single, we encourage you to find an accountability partner to help you keep on track. Find somebody you feel is mature and whom you know will be honest with you, someone who will challenge you toward excellence. Think of someone who's courageous enough to hold the Bible up to your face and say, "Look at the path you're following. It will have negative consequences!" When you're single, your accountability partner should be the same gender as you. Having an accountability partner of the opposite sex when you're not married breaks down the accountability very fast due to feelings, emotions, circumstances, pressures, motivations, or hidden agendas. Boyfriend and girlfriend, or even engaged couples, do not work well as accountability partners. The two people involved usually won't risk the relationship for honest truth or God's very best.

Be sure you don't overlook immediate sources of wisdom for an accountability partner. Consider asking your father to be your accountability partner, or ask an older person you respect to hold you accountable (again, someone who is the same gender as you).

PLUMB LINE PRINCIPLES
[The older women] can train the younger women.
—Titus 2:4a

If you're separated or divorced, and the father option is no longer available or feasible, find a godly accountability partner who may be in the same "season" of life as you. However, such an accountability partner should not provide the occasion as a weekly

Young men, in the same way be submissive to those who are older.
—1 Peter 5:5a

or monthly pity party or spouse bashing. Accountability meetings are intended for you to help each other and to cheer each other on to excellence.

For the young single man, this is a time for getting your career established, becoming financially prepared for a wife, and saving for a house. A mature accountability partner can help you keep on track, encourage you toward moral excellence, and be a mentor for spiritual growth.

For a married couple, our spouse is our accountability partner. This may mean we work on repairing communication lines, as discussed in chapter 5, "Master Bedroom." Other accountability partners, such as a financial planner or your minister, can be incorporated into the financial process as long as both partners have total peace about who is involved and everyone is clear about the purpose and objectives of seeking outside help.

Why is an accountability partner important? We all have blind spots that others can help us see and overcome. We also know how to rationalize our actions even to the point of deceiving ourselves. We need mentors to hold us accountable, to keep us on course toward what is the best and of the highest calling. Our goal should be to seek God's will for our lives. Accountability partners help us stay motivated toward spiritual and personal maturity.

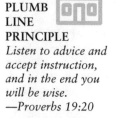

**PLUMB
LINE
PRINCIPLE**
*Listen to advice and
accept instruction,
and in the end you
will be wise.*
—Proverbs 19:20

4. Write Down Ideas

Our last safety instruction is that you write down your ideas, plans, and responsibilities. That's why we've included worksheets in the back for you to use. Some items relate to the big picture, the very important ongoing projects. Others relate to the little everyday errands. These may be two totally separate lists.

I (Dave) learned a long time ago from mentors like Gary Smalley, Gary Chapman, and Chuck Snyder (authors and relationship experts) to complete projects around the house in a timely fashion. These men helped me understand that the house and how it looks is an extension of my wife Debbie and is very important to her. This includes the little insignificant repairs that I tend to overlook or think, "I'll get to it later."

If Debbie has to keep after me every day to complete them, she feels she's nagging. In time, I start seeing it the same way. I then have a tendency to respond with negative words, expressions, and actions. So we learned long ago to handle this responsibility as follows: When Debbie sees a needed repair, she simply writes it down on a piece of paper and places it in my in-box. If it requires a certain completion date (like for an upcoming dinner party), she lets me know the date and time. I'm committed to getting these items done without further encouragement, unless I need clarification. If she doesn't write it down, chances are I won't remember to get around to it. I've learned that completing the project right away, or sooner than actually needed, helps Debbie feel extra special and that I place high honor on her and her needs.

If you're not already doing so, start your to-do list(s). Write things down, make any incremental steps measurable, and give yourself a due date. Ask yourself, "What is the goal and how do I get from point A to point B? What hurdles lie in front of me and how do I overcome them? What experts has God given me in my relationships or in my community who can help me overcome this obstacle or complete this project?"

Husbands, we encourage you to gently ask your wife to start giving you "honey-do" notes. Let her know that you will work hard to complete her list in a timely manner. You may need to ask forgiveness for past shortcomings, if this has been an area of contention.

Many weeks I have something on my honey-do list from Debbie. However, I look for the repairs so they're fixed even before she has a chance to write them down. It's so much fun to surprise her, and it makes her feel loved and appreciated. Men, let me add here that when you do this for your wife with pure motives and in an attitude of genuine love, there are unexpected ways she may reward you and reciprocate your love toward her.

Preparing the Ground (Rules)

PLUMB LINE PRINCIPLE
Finish your outdoor work and get your fields ready; after that, build your house.
—*Proverbs 24:27*

Before you build a house, proper preparation of the ground is very important. We need to establish some ground rules if we are going to get our financial house in good working order.

Level the Lot (Playing Field)

It's hard to build a solid foundation when the lot isn't properly prepared. One major aspect of this concept for married couples is what we refer to as "no more throwing rocks or dirt at each other."

Level the playing field. Go to your spouse and ask forgiveness for the things you've done in the past and make amends. Maybe you've made some financial mistakes. You overspent, or you haven't been totally honest with your spouse regarding a financial matter. Maybe you've run up the credit card balance, or you haven't revealed all of your income. If you want peace, then you have to confess these past and present mistakes and ask forgiveness.

Please recognize that you both must agree that it "takes two to tango"—you both made financial mistakes. No one spouse is totally innocent of all financial errors. You should confess your mistakes, and then each of you should agree to wipe the chalkboard clean.

You're probably aware of this "mistake chalkboard." It's not unusual for husbands and wives each to have one. When your spouse makes a mistake, you go to the mental chalkboard and write a tick mark on it next to the mistake. You add up these marks and say things like, "See, you always do this. Look how many times in our past you've done it" (pointing to the list and tallied tick marks).

PLUMB LINE PRINCIPLE
And be kind and compassionate to one another, forgiving one another, just as God also forgave you in Christ.
—Ephesians 4:32 HCSB

Sometimes it seems the wife's chalkboard gets used more often and the list is remembered longer. However, the man can have just as many marks on his chalkboard—he just doesn't verbalize them as much. His tick marks are silent and internal. Then when they surface, he may explode in an irrational way.

Husbands and wives, wipe the chalkboards clean and start with a clean slate. No more throwing rocks or dirt at each other.

I (Dave) want to share one very difficult, but truthful concept at this point. This truth may be hard for men to accept, especially those with broken marriages. However, we believe it to be a truth founded in Scripture and God's design for areas of responsibility within the marriage and between men and women.

Men come to me and say, "You don't understand what's going on in my marriage. My wife spends money like it grows on trees. She often goes out spending money we don't have and runs up bigger balances on our credit cards. She's sabotaging our finances. Our current financial difficulties are the result of my wife's actions and her irresponsibility."

When I hear this, I politely ask the wife to leave the room, if she's present. Then I turn to the husband, and my reply sounds something like this: "I'm sorry, but what have you done to your wife over the years that has so damaged your marriage relationship that your wife is now going out and spending money?

Women are security oriented; it goes against her very nature to sabotage the finances. You're reaping something you have sown. She must be feeling very unloved or demoralized at this time. Maybe you haven't handled the finances correctly in the past, or you aren't communicating with her enough. Have you loved her as deeply as Christ loved the church? Her actions are probably reactive and only a symptom of a real problem relating back to you and how you treat her."

Sometimes the husband replies, "But you still don't understand. She's not the same woman I married."

I answer, "You're right, and you helped create her! She was a beautiful, blossoming flower in your hand when you married her. Over the years you slowly squeezed the life out of her. She has closed up her spirit to you, and it's now manifested through her overspending. She is probably overspending so she can feel better about herself, even though it doesn't really bring the desired results."

Please understand, if your wife's spirit is closed to you, it doesn't mean the marriage is over. With love, patience, and care, her spirit can be opened again. Your relationship can be renewed, built back up to the love and passion you and she experienced when you were first married. Be aware that this process may take months or even years.

It has been said, and we believe this, that all marriage failures can be traced back to the husband. You may even have to go back to an event before the marriage, like being immoral prior to getting married (even if she agreed to engage in a sexual relationship with you). It is the man's responsibility to demonstrate godly leadership. Perhaps you didn't have the parents' complete consent to marry, or you didn't listen to their counsel. Maybe you didn't know your future wife long enough to learn about some personal issues in her background that today trigger problems and stresses. Be assured, however, that today's problems in your marriage can be traced back to some decision or choices you, the man, made, whether consciously or blindly (due to a lack of knowing or understanding his responsibilities or God's spiritual truths).

No matter what the circumstances, it's not too late to make changes now to save your relationship and, ultimately, your marriage. When this happens, God gets the glory, and we become a light and a testimony to others around us.

Clearing Away Obstacles and Debris

An important aspect of building or remodeling a financial house is to clear away any obstacles and debris lying around. These can trip you up and make you stumble, causing injury.

To clear away obstacles and level the ground, you must admit any hidden debts or obligations that your spouse doesn't know about. We mention this because it comes up in our seminars and in our years of counseling. One of the spouses has a hidden debt. He or she owes money to somebody, and the other spouse doesn't know about the debt. This money is usually owed to a friend, a coworker, or in the form of secret credit card balances.

If you're trying to get your financial house in order and there is still hidden debt(s), you must acknowledge the dishonesty that's been breeding within the relationship. It's absolutely devastating if discovered later, after the chalkboard has been cleared of all other offenses. Confess any hidden debts now and get all the financial facts out in the open. A marriage can't flourish when dishonesty festers under the surface.

Through marriage, God made the husband and wife one flesh. You're a team, even when struggling with each other. You need to move forward together, one day at a time, encouraging and helping each other every step of the way.

Beware of Greed

Another huge financial obstacle is greed. We want it all and we want it now. After all, it's the American way! We also say we want to be prosperous and obtain more so we can (supposedly) help others along the way. This is usually a misguided, and dare we say, untruthful motive. Usually, the bottom line is greed and covetousness. We want it first, and maybe if we make it big, we think we'll help others.

Let us share how we've seen this played out over our years of counseling others. People will come in for financial counseling because they're in dire financial straits. We can see they fell deeper in debt while pursuing a business in multilevel marketing. They tell us they got involved with multilevel marketing because they wanted to help others while helping themselves out of debt. The idea was to make more money so they could pay their debts, while also having more to give away.

What they don't realize as they explain this is that we're looking at their financial figures. It's clear they're not helping others now (or very sporadically). It's clear they got into debt serving their own needs and wants, living beyond their means. So we can't help wondering why they think they will give away more money when they make more? They're demonstrating a certain financial self-centeredness now and don't take care of others at this point; why would this change later? Is it easier to give away more money when you make more? Absolutely not! The more a person makes, the harder it can be to give. So in reality, their stated motive is probably not dealing in truth. It's a wonderful, noble goal. However, their bottom-line motive is probably more truthfully centered on greed—the desire to have more for themselves. Unfortunately, sometimes our Christian and church environments actually perpetuate such reasoning.

It's no mystery; greed gets people in trouble. Hey, we need to build a bigger barn. Right? Wrong. In Luke 12:13–34, Jesus answered the question, "Why are you building a bigger barn?" He said, "This very night your life will be demanded from you. Then who will get what you have prepared for yourself? *This is how it will be with anyone who stores up things for himself but is not rich toward God*" (vv. 20–21 emphasis added).

We live in a society that idolizes celebrities and millionaires with their bigger and better homes, cars, careers, and vacations. But bigger isn't always better.

Be careful of greed and its many trappings. Having a bigger house or the newest car may not be what your family really needs, or what God wants you to purchase. Understand, what size house you have doesn't matter to us. What really matters is

**PLUMB
LINE
PRINCIPLE**

*But godliness with contentment is great gain. For we brought nothing into the world, and we can take nothing out of it. But if we have food and clothing, we will be content with that. People who want to get rich fall into temptation and a trap and into many foolish and harmful desires that plunge men into ruin and destruction. For the love of money is a root of all kinds of evil. Some people, eager for money, have wandered from the faith and pierced themselves with many griefs.
—1 Timothy 6:6–10*

this: What is God's plan for your life and the money He entrusts to you?

Control Impulse Buying

Another big obstacle is impulse buying. This obstacle is very real to everyone, including us. No one is immune. Everybody is an impulse buyer; it simply boils down to the size and frequency of the impulses.

Contrary to popular belief, women are not the big impulse buyers—men are. A woman's impulse is to go down to the department store and buy a $200 dress the family can't afford. The man's impulse is to go out and buy a new car with a boat hanging on the back. The family can recuperate financially from the $200 dress. The family can't recuperate as easily from the thousands of dollars tied up in paying off the car and boat.

Most people have to work hard to control impulse buying. The Bible says, "If your right hand causes you to sin, cut it off" (Matt. 5:30a). That's a practical passage when it comes to impulse buying. Women, if you have a hard time controlling impulses in the area of clothes, shoes, and other apparel temptations, then quit visiting the mall. Men, if you have a hard time in the area of sporting goods, tools, and recreational items, quit hanging out at the hardware, sports, or superstores. If your credit cards cause you to stumble, cut them up!

Let's get very practical here. We've counseled many people who have had to make common sense, impulse-buying protection commitments (see below). If married, you both need to make these commitments together.

First, you should set a limit. Anything over this amount of money is now considered an impulse. The amount of money will depend on your personal financial situation.

Second, you agree that you won't buy anything on the spot. Get out of the store and give yourself a cooling-off period. That period may just be a realistic discussion with your spouse (if married), or it may be a period of time, like a day or a week. Most of us would be better off if we simply removed ourselves from the store and the temptation. Many times we wake up the next morning thinking, *That wouldn't have been the best purchase.* How many times have we all experienced buyer's remorse because we made an impulse purchase?

Each person needs to set into motion whatever it takes to control impulse buying. If credit cards are causing you to stumble, then cut them up or get them out of your pocket or purse. That doesn't mean that you can't place them back in your pocket at some later date. Life has seasons. We simply need to be realistic—and honest—about where we are financially and emotionally. Financial management is a discipline, and a discipline can be learned and improved over time.

In our family, who do you think is the big impulse buyer? Debbie? Wrong! I (Dave) am the big impulse buyer. Debbie is much more frugal and much more of a natural saver than I. I have to work at controlling impulses. I have to put up more boundaries than Debbie. Understand, the boundaries give our family freedom—freedom from financial bondage. This applies very specifically to impulse buying, but it also applies to all areas of finances.

PLUMB LINE PRINCIPLE
Turn my eyes away from worthless things; renew my life according to your word.
—Psalm 119:37

Each person, or couple, should apply whatever disciplines are necessary and set up needed boundaries in order to better control impulse buying, a very real obstacle to getting your financial house in order.

Freedom within Boundaries

How can boundaries create freedom? It may seem baffling, but it's a principle that truly works.

For instance, if you observe a day care with a playground near a busy road or freeway that has no fence, most of the children will huddle around the house when playing outside. They are aware and fearful of the cars and traffic.

However, if you construct a chain-link fence around the perimeter of the playground, the children feel total freedom to play right up to the fence. They will even lean and push against it; a few will want to violate the rules and climb on it. The fence creates a safe place for the children to play. They know there's comfort and safety within the boundaries.

The fence represents having a budget and establishing safe perimeters around our financial house—our spending and income. The fence gives us freedom to know the limits and enjoy the safety within. The fence is our personal financial truth. You see, budgeting reveals truth. The Bible tells us that you shall know the truth, and the truth will set you free (John 8:32).

This freedom within the walls is a concept many people don't see or grasp. People tend to think of budgeting as very confining. However, budgeting truly brings freedom—freedom with limits. And these limits aren't set in stone, never to be changed again. They're adjusted throughout our life as our financial picture changes.

Think about it—you will have more fun entertaining on $50 a month, if that's your limit, than spending $150 a month and having to look over your shoulder at the end of every month, wondering how you're going to pay off your Visa bill.

One difference in our analogy is that the day care's chain-link fence is strong and can withstand children pushing or leaning against it. But our financial fence is more like a paper-thin wall. If you push against it, your hand or whole body, will tear right through, usually resulting in stress and consumer debt.

Tearing a financial fence comes from impulse buying, over-spending, lack of planning, or using credit cards and other forms of consumer debt. Consumer credit allows us to live beyond our means and often starts a downward spiral into financial bondage (see chap. 4, "Laundry Room: Debt"). In counseling, we have never met anyone who likes being in financial bondage. Everyone hates it and wants to experience financial freedom—the freedom to enjoy the gifts of life, marriage, and family and the freedom to serve God more fully.

Learn to Be Content

The last obstacle we will address here is lack of contentment. The apostle Paul told us in Philippians 4:12–13, "I know what it is to be in need, and I know what it is to have plenty. I have learned the secret of being content in any and every situation, whether well fed or hungry, whether living in plenty or in want. I can do everything through him who gives me strength." We need to learn to be content in our financial circumstances as well as in all aspects of our lives.

But don't confuse *contentment* with *complacency*. Contentment is knowing that true happiness does not depend on material conditions. However, contentment should be balanced with responsibility. Be content with today's provisions, but strive to become better. The same Paul who advised us to be content also told us to run the race to win (1 Cor. 9:24)—that is, go for the prize! Let's run the race to win while at the same time learn to be content in our circumstances.

We'd like to share some examples. If you're an employee, you should be the best employee working for the company. You should be the one to show up on time, work honest hours, not take things home that don't belong to you, turn in honest expense reports, stop any gossip that may be traveling the halls, be an encourager to your coworkers, and talk positively about the company and any related problems.

If you're the best employee in the company, your employer should notice—and God can change your circumstances in due time through a raise, promotion, or new career opportunity.

If you honor God even in a job you dislike, He will make a way for you just as He did for Joseph (see Gen. 37, 39–41). Joseph was summoned from the dungeon where he'd been imprisoned on false charges in order to interpret Pharaoh's dream. Impressed with Joseph's wise, discerning counsel, Pharaoh said, "'Can we find anyone like this man, one in whom is the spirit of God?'" (Gen. 41:38). He promptly promoted

Joseph to a high position in Egypt, second in command only to Pharaoh himself—all because Joseph kept a godly, positive attitude and worked hard at all his tasks, no matter how unfair or dire his circumstances.

God may bless you with a raise or promotion. You could be offered new opportunities. If you feel locked into a dead-end position, continue "working for the Lord" (Col. 3:23), while keeping warm friendships with others in the industry. These contacts will see your positive character qualities and could be key in helping you find new and better opportunities. Understand, we're not advocating jumping ship every few months (loyalty is an important character trait as well). However, it's a reality today that employers are sometimes more interested in the bottom line than in the people who help produce it.

PLUMB LINE PRINCIPLE
Do not conform any longer to the pattern of this world, but be transformed by the renewing of your mind. Then you will be able to test and approve what God's will is—his good, pleasing and perfect will.
—Romans 12:2

If you are an employer, do you offer your products or services for a fair price? Do you take advantage of anyone in your business practices? Do you pay your employees a fair wage? Can they live on the wage you pay? Do you pay your suppliers and your taxes on time? Please consider this: If you are a Christian and a business owner with employees, you should strive to be the best employer in your market.

Lack of contentment is really greed in disguise. In fact, a major goal of the advertising world is to feed our sense of yearning, to solicit discontent so we will spend more money. Advertisements are designed for discontent. Instead, let's learn to be grateful for what we already have. Let's be content in our circumstances, giving thanks in all things. Don't confuse contentment with complacency, but let's work as if we're working for the Lord Himself (which in reality we are!).

Application

As you read these safety instructions and ground rules, what changes do you feel you need to start incorporating in your life and finances? What action steps do you need to write out and starting implementing in order to:

- Improve your prayer life?
- Study the Bible, especially as it relates to finances?
- Find and establish a mutual accountability partner?
- Level the ground or playing field (including asking forgiveness)?
- Clear up any unspoken hurts or hidden agenda?
- Work more as a team with your spouse (if married)?
- Eliminate the motive of greed and covetousness?
- Stop or reduce impulse buying?
- Quit striving after accumulating wealth and possessions (love of money)?
- Become more content in your circumstances (without becoming complacent)?

PLUMB LINE PRINCIPLE

He who loves pleasure will become poor.
—Proverbs 21:17a

Commit to the Lord whatever you do, and your plans will succeed.
—Proverbs 16:3

Go to the back of this book and write down your specific thoughts, convictions, goals, and action items. What time frames do you need to set? Who is going to hold you accountable to the process?

CHAPTER 3

FOYER/ENTRYWAY

Stewardship versus Ownership

Now this is what the Lord Almighty says:
"Give careful thought to your ways."
—HAGGAI 1:5

I n your financial house, the entryway is the beginning—the entrance or pathway—to all other areas of your finances. Let's review the master architect's design, the original blueprints for finances, as we discuss the difference between stewardship and ownership.

Many people are unaware that money is the second most talked about subject in the Bible. In fact, more than half of all the parables Jesus told His audiences dealt with the topic of money. Do you know why? Money is often the testing ground of our choices, our character, and even our theology. Luke 16:10–11 says, "Whoever can be trusted with very little can also be trusted with much, and whoever is dishonest with very little will also be dishonest with much. So if you have not been trustworthy in handling worldly wealth, who will trust you with true riches?" At the end of verse 13, we read, "You cannot serve both God and Money." In a most amazing way, money is a tangible indicator of our true relationship with God. In fact, our bank and credit card statements provide an exact index of our lives.

In the seminars we teach, we like to tell attendees that if someone was willing, we could project his or her checkbook ledger on the screen up front and take an intimate look into that person's life. Of course, no one would volunteer to do that. But here's the point: If we could look into your checkbook, we'd probably know what size house you live in, what kind of cars you drive, what kind of pets you have, where you go out for dinner, what your hobbies and vices are, and what your giving habits are. We'd know everything about you. See, money is nothing more than an exact index of your life that tells you and me right where you are with God. Your checkbook tells it all.

Is there a relationship between faith and finance? It's easy to say that God is Lord of our lives, but for many it's not really true until we allow Him to be Lord of our finances.

What Does the Bible Say?

God owns everything:

- "To the LORD your God belong the heavens, even the highest heavens, the earth and everything in it" (Deut. 10:14).
- "Yours, O LORD, is the greatness and the power and the glory and the majesty and the splendor, for everything in heaven and earth is yours. Yours, O LORD, is the kingdom; you are exalted as head over all. Wealth and honor come from you; you are the ruler of all things. In your hands are strength and power to exalt and give strength to all" (1 Chron. 29:11–12).
- "The earth is the Lord's, and everything in it, the world, and all who live in it" (Ps. 24:1).
- "Every animal of the forest is mine, and the cattle on a thousand hills. I know every bird in the mountains, and the creatures of the field are mine. If I were hungry I would not tell you, for the world is mine, and all that is in it" (Ps. 50:10–11).
- "Who has a claim against me that I must pay? Everything under heaven belongs to me" (Job 41:11).

- "'The silver is mine and the gold is mine,' declares the LORD Almighty" (Hag. 2:8).
- "Do you not know that your body is a temple of the Holy Spirit, who is in you, whom you have received from God? You are not your own; you were bought at a price. Therefore honor God with your body" (1 Cor. 6:19–20).

In Exodus 19:5, God claims the whole earth. In Leviticus 25:23, He claims the land; in Psalm 50:10 the beasts, the cattle, the birds; in Deuteronomy 10:14 and Psalm 89:11, God claims both the heaven and the earth; in Haggai, He claims the silver and gold; and in 1 Corinthians, He claims ownership of us.

Can there be any doubt Who owns it all?

What Is Stewardship?

A steward could be described as someone who manages someone else's resources. Your banker is a steward. You take your money to your banker and give it to him. You say, "Take care of this money. When I return, I expect the money back with interest."

Now think about the banker. When the banker takes your money, he has certain responsibilities and privileges. He has the privilege of building buildings with the money, investing it, paying an electric bill, and paying employees with it. He has certain privileges.

However, if your banker calls you one day from Hawaii at his beachfront house, in his Mercedes, on his cellular phone, and says, "You know those withdrawal slips you've been filling out? Don't fill out any more, because there's no money left—I spent it all." Obviously, this banker switched from a *steward* to an *owner*. That's exactly what you and I do. We switch from being *stewards* to being *owners*, perhaps never even understanding this principle. We consume it all and say, "God, there's no money left."

Understanding the principle of stewardship is realizing everything belongs to God and that we're managers of His resources. When we accept our role as stewards, every spending decision becomes a spiritual one. We no longer pray, "Lord, how should I manage my money?" but we pray, "Lord, how do You want me to manage *Your* money?"

Let's review Luke 16:10–11 again. Jesus said, "Whoever can be trusted with very little can also be trusted with much, and whoever is dishonest with very little will also be dishonest with much. So if you have not been trustworthy in handling worldly wealth, who will trust you with true riches?"

God wants to entrust us with "true riches," which go beyond money. If we aren't trustworthy with a little thing like money, how can He trust us with bigger things? There is no better indicator of our goals and values in life than in how we acquire, use, and manage the money and resources in our care.

PLUMB LINE PRINCIPLE
Let a man regard us in this manner, as servants of Christ and stewards of the mysteries of God. In this case, moreover, it is required of stewards that one be found trustworthy.
—1 Corinthians 4:1–2
NASB

The Principle of Sowing and Reaping

God uses another principle in finances that's also evident in our physical world: the principle of cause and effect, or more familiarly, sowing and reaping.

- "The wicked man earns deceptive wages, but he who sows righteousness reaps a sure reward" (Prov. 11:18).
- "As I have observed, those who plow evil and those who sow trouble reap it" (Job 4:8).
- "Do not be deceived: God cannot be mocked. A man reaps what he sows. The one who sows to please his sinful nature, from that nature will reap destruction; the one who sows to please the Spirit, from the Spirit will reap eternal life" (Gal. 6:7–8).

If you sow irresponsibility, you will reap financial havoc. Many times in counseling we got the same type of phone call. For example, a lady called our office one day and she was crying. She described her family's circumstances, and when she finished, she said, "How could God let this happen to us?" I (Dave) lovingly told this lady, "Ma'am, God has nothing to do with this. Your family is simply reaping what it sowed." I explained God's view of money and our responsibility to manage it. If, like in her family's situation, we sow irresponsibility, we must confess it, make restitution (pay off the debt), and move ahead. God will walk with us through the valley, or in rare cases He may choose to deliver us from the valley, but that's His decision. We need to be faithful to our responsibility.

Let's take a step back to see a bigger picture of what's going on in our country from a biblical perspective. One of the major problems today is the national debt. We are now more than $5 trillion in debt. Does that mean anything to you? It doesn't to us. It's easy to say $5 trillion. How much is a trillion dollars? Here's a word picture we learned from Larry Burkett. If you took a pile of $1,000 bills and tightly stacked them to make a million dollars, your stack would be about four inches high. If you stack up a billion dollars in $1,000 bills, your stack just grew to about 333 feet high, about as tall as the Statue of Liberty. If you stack up a trillion dollars in $1,000 bills, your stack is now sixty-three miles high. See, we don't have a clue as to what we've done as a nation. Now we can visualize the problem and take it seriously. It will take a nation turning back to God and His biblical principles in order to solve it.

Let's look at Deuteronomy 28. This was written to the nation of Israel, but we can see a snapshot of the United States here too.

"Now it shall be, if you diligently obey the LORD your God, being careful to do all His commandments which I command you today, the LORD your God will set you high above all the nations of the earth. All these blessings will come upon you and overtake you if you obey the LORD your God" (vv. 1–2 NASB). See, God is saying, if you obey Me as a nation, here's what you're going to look like as a nation, described further in verses 12–13: "The LORD will open for you His good storehouse, the heavens, to give rain to your land in its season and to bless all the work of your hand; and you shall lend to many nations, but you shall not borrow. The LORD will make you the head and not the tail, and you only will be above, and you will not be underneath." Doesn't this sound like the United States for the past two hundred years? One nation, under God. Despite what you hear on the news today, despite what you read in your kids' history books, our founding fathers lived by biblical principles, even if they didn't claim to be Christians—and God prospered them.

Verse 15: "But it shall come about, if you will not obey the LORD your God, to observe to do all of His commandments and His statutes with which I charge you today, that all these curses will come upon you and overtake you." He describes what a nation will look like if we choose not to obey Him. Go to verses 43–44: "The alien who is among you shall rise above you higher and higher, but you will go down lower and lower. He shall lend to you, but you will not lend to him; he will be the head, and you will be the tail." The United States is now the largest debtor nation in the world. We owe more money than all other nations put together.

If we look closely, we can see in these verses that the problem in our country is not the national debt. Debt is simply a symptom of the real problem. The real problem is, as a nation, we've turned our back on God. We've taken God out of government. We've taken God out of our judicial system. In 1962, we took God out of public schools. And in many places across this nation, right now we're in the process of taking God out of the church.

When a nation turns its back on God, natural consequences result. One is we're a nation in debt. We're suffering under that consequence right now. But we also believe that if we apply God's principles to our lives, we can reap the blessings of God's promises by following His principles. We can be debt free. And we believe this can include our houses being free of a mortgage.

"What?" you say. "You have to have a mortgage to buy a house!" Consider this: In 1928, only 2 percent of the houses in America had mortgages. Today, over 60 percent of all the houses in America are mortgaged. Who changed, God? No, we changed. Understand, sixty years ago, you would have been embarrassed to tell anybody you had a mortgage on your house. Who changed, God? No, we changed. In our financial seminars we go through a detailed scenario with the attendees, explaining how we are only one generation away from paying cash for houses. It takes just one disciplined generation to stop the debt cycle—even on real estate.

What if we got back to the vision God has for us? What if we got back to following His principles? Financial freedom is not just freedom from debt but also freedom to bless others with our abundance, freedom to go where God calls us to go, and freedom to make a difference! Imagine the impact on our world if we would control our desires in the area of finances. What we sow, we shall reap.

Second Chronicles 7:14 says, "If my people, who are called by my name, will humble themselves and pray and seek my face and turn from their wicked ways, then will I hear from heaven and will forgive their sin and will heal their land." For many years we've spent time on our knees praying, "Lord, heal this nation. Bring this nation back to You." We thought that's what that passage meant.

When I (Dave) attended Promise Keepers in Washington, D.C., I was lying prostrate on the ground with the other million men, burdened and praying for our country, when God dealt with me. He reminded me that the verse says, "If *My* people who are called by *My* name will humble themselves, I'll heal the land" (emphasis added, paraphrased). The problem is not out there in the world; the problem is right here, with you and with me. If we, as Christians, will humble ourselves and seek God, God will take care of the people in leadership in this country as well as those who don't know or follow Him. He will heal the land in a way that we can't see today because He's God.

So the next time you hear news about the national debt, pray for our leaders, and pray for the Christian community, but remember to check your heart. Have you humbled yourself before God, and have you sought His face?

God's Economy

What is the key to stewardship and financial freedom? Our attitudes about money and material possessions.

Second Corinthians 8:14 says, "At the present time your plenty will supply what they need, so that in turn their plenty will supply what you need."

This is God's economy. Not that we take our money, pool it together, and live in a commune, but that each of us follow God's principles. Then, when you have a need, God taps me on the shoulder to meet your need.

PLUMB LINE PRINCIPLE

If My people, who are called by my name, will humble themselves and pray and seek my face and turn from their wicked ways, then will I hear from heaven and will forgive their sin and will heal their land.
—*2 Chronicles 7:14*

And when I have a need, God taps you on the shoulder to meet my need. However, if we're not paying attention to what God says about managing money, we aren't available to do so, and the needs go unmet.

In teaching seminars we know that someone in the audience is probably worried about how she or he is going to make the next rent or house payment. We also know there's probably somebody else in the audience who has the money to make that payment. Please understand, we're not talking about the need of someone who's acting irresponsibly, a topic we address more fully in chapter 6, "Dining Room." But in cases of genuine need, people remain isolated, they are not applying God's principles, the need goes unmet, *and God is not glorified.*

This whole book pivots on this truth that God is the owner of it all. But we as individuals and families struggle with this concept because there's a checkbook in our pocket with our name on it, and there's a car out there with our name on it, and we live in a house that's got our name on it, and we've got a bank account with our name on it. Remember, God's Word makes clear that He is the owner of all. He owns all of our stuff. He owns your bank account, your pension, your investments, and your IRA. And John 3:27 says, "A man can receive only what is given him from heaven." God is the owner of it all, and what we have, He provides.

Stewardship in the Bible

PLUMB LINE PRINCIPLE

Give me neither poverty nor riches, but give me only my daily bread. Otherwise, I may have too much and disown you and say, "Who is the Lord?" Or I may become poor and steal, and so dishonor the name of my God.
—Proverbs 30:8b–9

The role God gives us is one of stewardship. We defined a steward as someone who manages someone else's resources.

One of the greatest passages in the Bible dealing with stewardship is in Matthew 25. Christ was talking to His disciples, and He'd been trying to tell them, "I'm going back to my Father," but they didn't understand, so He told them a parable:

"It will be like a man going on a journey, who called his servants and entrusted his property to them" (v. 14). Christ knew He was going on a journey, and because He's God, He's the owner of it all, and He's entrusted portions of it to you and me.

"To one he gave five talents of money, to another two talents, and to another one talent, each according to his ability. Then he went on his journey" (v. 15).

That's an important passage to understand. God does the entrusting according to our ability. If we've got our eyes on each other, that causes problems. If I'm watching my neighbor over here and he's a little bit better off than I am financially, and I look on him with a little bit of envy, the Bible calls that coveting—and that's sin. Or maybe I'm watching my neighbor over there, and I see I'm doing a little bit better than he is financially, and I may begin to look down on him a little and let that fuel my ego, but the Bible calls that pride—and that's sin. That's why our eyes must be focused on Jesus Christ (Heb. 12:2). Not on the person living on my right or my left, not the person in the pew to my right or my left, but on Jesus Christ. He does the entrusting according to our ability. We just need to be found faithful in managing what He's entrusted to us.

"The man who had received the five talents went at once and put his money to work and gained five more. So also, the one who with the two talents gained two more. But the man who had received the one talent went off, dug a hole in the ground and hid his master's money. After a long time the master of those servants returned and settled accounts with them" (Matt. 25:16–19).

That's an important passage. For those of us who know Jesus Christ as our personal Savior, that has to be one of the most sobering passages in the Bible regarding money because there's coming a day when we will stand before the almighty God and be required to tell Him how we managed His money. That's a serious thought, as we walk through life doing *what* we want, *when* we want, and really not taking into account God's kingdom and His biblical purposes.

Now if you do not know Jesus Christ as your personal Savior, this passage does not apply to you. When you meet your Maker face-to-face, He's not going to ask you one thing about money. The only thing He's going to ask you is, "What did you do with My Son, Jesus Christ?" Our hope is when that day comes, you have the right answer: "I accepted Him as my personal Lord and Savior."

The Parable of the Talents

The man who had received the five talents brought the other five. "Master," he said, "you entrusted me with five talents. See, I have gained five more." His master replied, "Well done, good and faithful servant! You have been faithful with a few things; I will put you in charge of many things. Come and share your master's happiness!" The man with the two talents also came. "Master," he said, "you entrusted me with two talents; see, I have gained two more." His master replied, "Well done, good and faithful servant! You have been faithful with a few things; I will put you in charge of many things. Come and share your master's happiness!" (Matt. 25:20–23).

Did you notice that these two servants had different amounts of money, but the reward was the same? It's not the *amount* of money we have that's important but our *attitude* about the money. That's what God cares about.

"Then the man who had received the one talent came. 'Master,' he said, 'I knew that you are a hard man, harvesting where you have not sown and gathering where you have not gathered seed. So I was afraid and went out and hid your talent in the ground. See, here is what belongs to you'" (vv. 24–25).

Notice he said, "I was afraid." Fear caused this man to think and do things in a way that is not consistent with God's nature. We should not be fearful, and that includes being fearful of the financial areas of our lives.

> His master replied, "You wicked, lazy servant! So you knew that I harvest where I have not sown and gather where I have not scattered seed? Well then, you should have put my money on deposit with the bankers, so that when I returned I would have received it back with interest. Take the talent from him and give it to the one who has the ten talents. For everyone who has will be given more, and he will have an abundance. Whoever does not have, even what he has will be taken from him. And throw that worthless servant outside, into the darkness, where there will be weeping and gnashing of teeth" (vv. 26–30).

Notice two things here in these verses. One is a reference to conservative investing (that is, putting money on deposit with the bankers). This is probably something we all may wish we had understood sooner, or done more wisely with the volatility of the stock market. The second is a message about stewardship: Use it for God's work and glory or lose it. In addition, if we don't manage it with the Master's best interests in mind, we risk consequences. God calls us to be stewards, not owners.

Consider this: Although essential to an obedient walk with God, stewardship is one of the last issues a Christian may deal with in his or her relationship with Him. We are willing to turn over a lot of areas to God before we will turn over our checking account to Him.

You cannot deal with true stewardship in your life until you first deal with lordship. Who is lord of your life? Christ and His Word, or you and your own thoughts and beliefs? Take an honest inventory right now. Who is in charge? What does your schedule from last week reflect about who or what is lord of your life? What about your calendar for the coming week? For most of us, this issue of lordship is an ongoing struggle.

Understand, you can't deal with stewardship or the issue of lordship in your life until you first deal with your personal relationship with Jesus Christ. Look at this last verse again: "And throw that worthless servant outside, into the darkness, where there will be weeping and gnashing of teeth." If you go through the Gospels, that verse appears several times, describing eternal separation from God, which we can call hell. That means there's an even more important message in here than stewardship: our personal relationship with Jesus Christ.

Look at this parable from another perspective. The first servant took in God's Word and accepted Jesus Christ as his personal Savior. He then acted upon his changed life and used the gifts God gave him to bear fruit for God's kingdom work twofold. The second servant also took in God's Word, accepted Christ, acted upon his changed life, and used his God-given gifts to bear fruit for God's kingdom work twofold. This increase doesn't happen by accident, nor by simply warming a pew every Sunday. God has a ministry for every Christian. You need to find that ministry, both at your local church and in your community, and allow God to do His work through your life.

Don't be like the third servant. He took in God's Word. He went to church often. Maybe he taught Sunday school classes and attended leadership meetings. When the offering plate went by, he probably put in some money, maybe even tithes and offerings. This guy knew all about God. However, he didn't have a personal relationship with the Master (Jesus Christ), and he was cast into the outer darkness where there's weeping and gnashing of teeth (v. 30).

Many people know about God and even attend church regularly. Maybe this describes you too. However, do you have a *personal* relationship with Jesus Christ? If not, or if you have any doubts, now is the time to get right with God by asking Jesus Christ into your heart to be your personal Savior. Remember, "The earth is the LORD's, and everything in it, the world, and all who live in it" (Ps. 24:1). Jesus said, "For my Father's will is that everyone who looks to the Son and believes in Him shall have eternal life" (John 6:40). He also said, "I am the way, and the truth, and the life; no one comes to the Father but through Me" (John 14:6 NASB).

After you settle your personal relationship with Jesus Christ, then you next need to deal with this important issue of lordship. Who is Lord of your life, Christ and His written Word (the Bible) or you and your thoughts? When you settle the question, Who is in charge? then you are ready to work on the next step, which is the matter of stewardship.

PLUMB LINE PRINCIPLE

Let not a rich man boast of his riches; but let him who boasts boast of this, that he understands and knows Me.
—Jeremiah 9:23b–24 NASB

From Owners to Stewards

Years ago, when we first heard this message of stewardship, we said to ourselves, "Who are we kidding? We're not stewards." Although we were Christians, we recognized that we clearly acted as "owners" and just put some of "our" money in the offering plate each payday.

So that night we went home and knelt down at the foot of our bed to pray. For us, our bed that night was like the Old Testament altar. Altars were used for sacrifices. In obedience to God, Abraham offered his only son Isaac on an altar. (The angel of the Lord stopped him, and God provided a ram for the sacrifice. See the whole story in Gen. 22.)

God was saying, "Do you love Me, or do you just say you love Me?"

That night we knelt down at our bed and started putting stuff on the altar. *We put our house on the altar, Lord. It's not our house but Your house.* We also placed on the altar our perceived right to be "homeowners." We even put on the altar the equity in the house. *Not our equity, Lord—Your equity.*

Next we put on the altar our cars. *Lord, You know we need to get back and forth to work and other places to do the things we need to do, but if You make clear to us these cars belong to somebody else, we'll give them away.* Three times God has said to us, "Do you mean it?" Three times God has directed us to give our cars away to someone more in need.

We also put on the altar our bank accounts that night. At the time, there wasn't much in them, but we said, *Lord, here they are. The money is Yours.*

We even put our children on the altar that night. The Lord never promised any of us parents a full life with our kids; He's just entrusted them to us for a season. So we gave our children and our perceived parental rights back to the Lord.

We put a lot of things on the altar that night.

PLUMB LINE PRINCIPLE
None of you can be My disciple who does not give up all his own possessions.
—Luke 14:33 NASB

However, something interesting happens when you give up ownership like this. While your right hand is putting things on the altar before the Lord, what's your left hand doing? It's coming up to grab those things back. You see, stewardship is a daily process. For some, it may be minute by minute. The Bible says, "I stay close to you; your right hand upholds me" (Ps. 63:8). That keeps us out of His affairs.

What do you need to place on the altar? What do you need to lay at God's feet? Are you a steward or an owner? Listen, we're no different from you. We can lay it on the altar, and ten minutes later we're running with it again. This is an ongoing, day-by-day process. In fact, this is such an important point, we'd like to stop and pray with you about this right now— because if you don't deal with these issues, none of the rest is going to matter.

- If you know about God but you know you don't have an intimate, personal relationship with His Son, Jesus Christ, and you now want to get right with God, pray this prayer:

Father, I realize my life is not right with You. I want to know You. Please forgive me for my sin. I now invite Jesus Christ into my life as my personal Savior. You promised to dwell in me and give me eternal life. Help me learn to follow You in every area of my life. Thank You, Lord. Now go tell someone (another Christian, a pastor, etc.) that you just prayed to receive Christ as your personal Savior. That person will help you take the next steps in your walk with God.

PLUMB LINE PRINCIPLES

One thing God has spoken, two things have I heard: that you, O God, are strong, and that you, O Lord, are loving. Surely You will reward each person according to what he has done.
—Psalm 62:11–12

Then I acknowledged my sin to you and did not cover up my iniquity. I said, "I will confess my transgressions to the Lord"— and you forgave the guilt of my sin.
—Psalm 32:5

• If you have already received Christ as your personal Savior, but somewhere along the way you've removed Christ from the throne of your life so you now sit on the throne and run your life your way, pray this prayer: *Father, I now realize my life is not right with You. Even though I'm a Christian and placed my faith in Jesus Christ, and I go to church and do good things, I know I've been running my life my way, not by your Word and principles. I need to put Jesus first in my life. Please forgive me for my willful and disobedient spirit. I now place Jesus Christ back on the throne of my life and purpose to follow Him from now on. Thank You for loving me and receiving me back unconditionally. Help me follow through in this commitment for the rest of my life. Thank You, Lord, for loving me so much. I pray this in the name of Jesus Christ. Amen.*

• If you're a Christian and you already love the Lord and acknowledge His lordship in your life but you haven't dealt with this issue of stewardship, then pray this prayer: *Father, I now recognize that although I love You, and I give money faithfully, and I serve in many ways at my church, I recognize that I have been acting as an owner, not a steward. I need to put everything on the altar—my house and my right to be a homeowner, the equity in the house, my bank accounts, my cars, my investments, my marriage, my children. And Lord, I have a box full of bills, so I place that on the altar, knowing You even paid the price for my lack of discipline. I give it all to You, Lord. I purpose that I will seek Your will in how to manage these things, from this day forward. Thank You, Lord, for loving me so much. I pray this in the name of Jesus Christ. Amen.*

Now we would like to pray for you: *Father, as we bring our prayers before You for all these things You are laying on our hearts through Your Holy Spirit, please give us the grace to follow through. Lord, we don't ask for the grace for the next year because we can't go that long, but give us the grace for the next half hour and the next hour after that, so we will be obedient to Your Word. We ask this in the name and through the blood and resurrection of Jesus Christ and for His sake. Amen.*

Application

What has God been talking to you about as you read this chapter?

What changes do you need to make?

When will you start your new plan?

CHAPTER 4

LAUNDRY ROOM

Debt

Show me the way I should go,
for to you I lift up my soul.
—PSALM 143:8B

When we think about the laundry room from a financial perspective, we think about the stains of debt. In reading this book, you will learn how to wash away old habits that are not in line with God's Word. We will also answer some of the most often asked questions. What does God's Word say about debt and borrowing? What about credit cards? What are some of the consequences of debt? If you're in debt, how can you become financially free? We will look at these areas of debt from a biblical perspective. But first, let's define the problem.

Did you know:

- Adults spend more time shopping each week than they spend with their children.
- More Americans visit shopping malls on Sunday than go to church.
- More Americans file for bankruptcy each year than graduate from college.
- The average American home is more than twice as large as it was in the 1950s, yet the average family is smaller.

- We work longer hours, have less time for families, and are more stressed out.[1]

Like the five stages of grief, we go through similar stages in dealing with debt:

1. Denial: "I don't have any money problems, but I need help."
2. Anger: "It's not my fault. My creditors are to blame. I'm a victim!"
3. Bargaining: "Debt consolidation—I'll never get in trouble again."
4. Depression: "My situation is hopeless. What am I going to do?"
5. Acceptance: "I am responsible. I will do whatever it takes to solve my problem."

Debt is a major problem today. America's families suffer from an epidemic of "affluenza," acquiring things at a staggering pace, with devastating consequences. Personal bankruptcies filed each year soared from 874,000 in 1995 to 1.573 million by the first quarter of 2003.[2] Consumer debt has reached a historic high, now equaling 101 percent of income.[3] Americans carry an average credit card balance of $12,000 per household.[4]

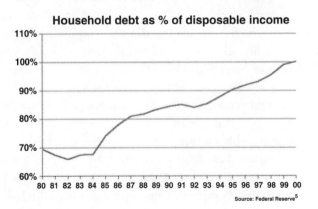

Household debt as % of disposable income

Source: Federal Reserve[5]

In addition, we Americans do not save money as in prior years. Ten years ago, families in the United States saved about 9 percent of disposable income. Today that figure has plunged to zero.[6] Proverbs 13:11 says, "Wealth hastily gotten will dwindle, but he who gathers it little by little will increase it." However, our culture slowly turned from saving money to increased consumption (and debt). This trend continued during the economic recession of 2001, subsequent job losses, and in the wake of the terrorist attacks on America on September 11, 2001.

In 2001, Barna Research compiled the following information about debt and Americans' perception of money:

- Thirty-seven percent of Americans report they are "in debt" (2000).
- Thirty-two percent of adults report that they personally struggle with finances (2001).
- Thirty-three percent of born-again Christians say it is impossible for them to get ahead in life because of the financial debt they have incurred (1997).[7]

What Does God's Word Say about Borrowing and Debt?

There are two major schools of thought on what the Bible says about borrowing and debt. One is based on Romans 13:8, "Owe no man anything except the debt of love." We don't totally agree with this singular, no-debt-ever position because the Bible gives many other verses, guidelines, and principles related to lending and borrowing. We believe this one verse does not encompass the whole counsel of God on the subject.

The second school of thought recognizes that God's Word describes a range that we are free to operate within regarding many subjects. This includes financial matters. Remember, we mentioned earlier that what is a freedom for you may not be a freedom for us, and what is a freedom for us may not be a freedom for you, and both can be in God's will (Rom. 14:2–8). In this chapter, we will examine debt from the perspective of a "range of economy."

In God's range of economy, what does He say about borrowing and debt? "The wicked borrows and does not pay back" (Ps. 37:21 NASB). God's minimum standard is clear: If you borrow money, you must pay it back—even if it takes you the rest of your life.

This may seem extreme in light of a simple and easy legal remedy such as bankruptcy. In fact, bankruptcy has become so prevalent in our society that it's now viewed as normal and acceptable. Understand, if you are so backed into a corner financially that you can't think, can't sleep, can't eat, can't work—basically, that you can't carry on with life, then you may need to seek the shelter of the bankruptcy act.

However, for the Christian, bankruptcy should be the last option, not the first. And if we must seek the shelter of bankruptcy, we must purpose to pay the money back—even if takes us the rest of our lives. If we don't purpose to pay the money back, we'll never do it. With God's help, we can complete that goal, and He will build within us a testimony the rest of the world will want to hear. In fact, if we honor God by paying back what we owe, God may honor us by opening doors for us to share that testimony, which reveals His grace and brings Him glory.

PLUMB LINE PRINCIPLE
No one can serve two masters. Either he will hate the one and love the other, or he will be devoted to the one and despise the other. You cannot serve both God and Money.
—Matthew 6:24

During one of our seminars, a lady came forward during a break. She appeared very distressed. "My husband and I are in a mess," she said. "We have to file for bankruptcy. We don't have any other options. We've already been to an attorney."

I (Dave) asked for specifics. "How much do you have in credit card debt?"

She answered in an overwhelmed tone, "About $12,000."

Clearly, to her that was a lot of money. However, having done a lot of financial counseling, we've stared across the table at $150,000 in credit card debt. I listened as she continued. Her husband had been out of work for awhile. This created a serious cash-flow problem. I asked if they also had a car payment, and she said, "No, we drive two beaters, and they get us around town all right."

"Are you renting?" I asked.

"No, we're buying a house."

"What's the house worth, conservatively?"

She paused to think a moment and answered, "About $275,000."

"What do you owe on the house?"

"About $225,000," she replied.

I asked if they had a second mortgage or any liens on the property, and she shook her head no.

At that point I gently replied, "Ma'am, you and your husband have the money to pay off your credit card debt; you just don't realize it. If you were truly serious about paying what you owe, you could sell your house, pay the money back out of the equity, and start over." She didn't like hearing this, but she and her husband had not truly considered all the options available to them.

What if someone has a high amount of credit card debt, but they don't have a house they could sell to pay off this debt, and they're committed to the idea that bankruptcy is not an option? What can they do? Many times the first thing someone in this situation does is contact an agency like Consumer Credit Counseling Service or others like it. That's why agencies like that exist, to see what they can do to get debt payments reduced. Retailers created such agencies—they would rather get some money back than nothing. You could try talking to your creditors yourself. Banks have the right to forgive the debt or reduce the interest. Of course, they may not, but it's at least worth a phone call. If you can't make contact or they won't cooperate, then seek outside help.

Over the years many people have come to us convinced their only option was bankruptcy after Consumer Credit Counseling Service or other agencies concluded they could not help. When we asked why CCCS couldn't help, the client usually responded, "They said we don't make enough money to cover the minimum payments and also pay our current monthly expenses."

At that point we usually ask, "How much are you short each month? How much more do you need to pay the creditors every month?" Let's say they answer, "Four hundred dollars per month." We then ask, "How can you go out and generate that extra $400? You created this amount of debt, but your income is at this level, so how can you increase your income to pay your creditors?"

Sometimes they simply need help thinking outside the box. What assets can they sell? Who else can help? What about family? Can either spouse work a part-time job until the debt is paid off? These are tough, but necessary, questions. The point is that bankruptcy should be the last option, not the first option.

PLUMB LINE PRINCIPLE
*Do not worry then, saying "What will we eat?" or "What will we drink?" or "What will we wear for clothing?"... For your heavenly Father knows that you need all these things.
—Matthew 6:31–32
NASB*

Let's face it—life can be just plain tough. We experience devastating emergencies or unexpected circumstances beyond our control. As a result we are "forced" into bankruptcy. However, based upon God's Word, we must purpose to pay back the money we borrowed, no matter how long it takes. If you've already gone through bankruptcy, consider setting aside $10 a month or more toward paying back your creditors someday, in order to fulfill the biblical principle of paying back what is owed. However, please be aware that you cannot simply start sending one of your creditors $10 per month. If you do, you may negate your bankruptcy and reactivate the promissory notes with your creditors. There are specific laws and guidelines regarding such matters, so to understand them, please seek knowledgeable legal counsel (hopefully Christian) before you repay debts that were dismissed in your bankruptcy proceedings. Think of the incredible testimony you would have if God helped you fulfill your goal of repaying all your creditors!

Now that we've discussed the minimum standard we see in God's Word—to pay what we owe—what is the other side of God's economic range?

Philippians 4:19 says, "And my God will meet all your needs according to his glorious riches in Christ Jesus." The idea here is no debt at all. We can trust God to provide for us. We should take care of our responsibilities, and God will take care of our needs. The key to God's principles of finance is somewhere within this range.

The Debt Mentality

If you struggle with debt, recognize that you may also be subject to a "debt mentality":

- Believing you need more than God has provided for you to have.
- Believing God doesn't know best what your needs are.
- Believing God has failed to provide for your needs, forcing you to take matters into your own hands.
- Presuming upon God that since today's income may be sufficient to make debt payments, so will tomorrow's.

Biblical Warnings about Debt

Debt in the Bible is always presented in a negative context, never in a positive light. One of God's warnings appears in Proverbs 22:7, "The rich rule over the poor, and the borrower is servant to the lender." This is one of God's steadfast principles. If you borrow money from anybody for any reason, this principle goes into effect, whether you like it, believe it, or choose to ignore it.

Financial counselors never have to explain the words *servitude* or *bondage* to anybody in counseling. Clients understand exactly what this means when they're in financial trouble. Some can't eat, can't sleep, can't think, and can't work. And so the counselor doesn't have to explain the principle of becoming the lender's slave, because the client is living it.

Be aware, however, that even if you're buying a house using debt and you make enough money to cover the house payment, this principle of servitude goes into effect automatically. First, you have to continue making a certain salary to pay those mortgage payments. Second, you have to keep up the maintenance of the house or property, which also costs money. And third, if one day God says, "I have a mission for you," you're not as free to pick up and go. Not a lot of us entertain such a possibility, but if we are truly yielded to God's will for us, this should be a consideration. However, with a mortgage, we are tied to the house, its maintenance, and those payments. There is always servitude with debt.

What about lending money to family members, such as adult children? Does this principle apply then as well?

Considering Proverbs 22:7, we would answer yes. When we lend money to our children, the relationship shifts. It may be imperceptible at first, but here's what happens:

Your grown children come to you with a financial need and ask to borrow money. You think, *I want to help.* And so you lend them the money. As time goes by, you may find yourself thinking, *You know, the kids don't come over nearly as much as they used to. I wonder why?* You may not see it, but you sense it—the dynamic between you and your children has changed.

As for your children, they're saying, "You know, every time we go over to Mom and Dad's, the subject of money seems to come up. It's like they want to put in their two cents' worth of opinion on every dime we spend. I feel like they watch every move we make. It's not as much fun to go to their house for dinner anymore." Your children feel the scrutiny, even if unintentional, because of this principle that the borrower is servant to the lender. Additionally, if there are any hardships in the kids' finances, they will withdraw.

You see, the lender feels no bondage (you just wanted to help), but the Bible is clear; the borrower becomes a servant to the lender. As soon as the transaction occurred, the relationship changed from parent-child to lender-borrower. What's the definition of a distant relative? A close relative who owes you money.

Understand, we're not saying that you should never lend money to your children. It could work out just fine. However, be aware of this biblical principle and the dynamic that's added to your parent-child relationship.

Consequences of Debt

PLUMB LINE PRINCIPLE
The rich rules over the poor, and the borrower becomes the lender's slave.
—Proverbs 22:7
NASB

Debt results when we borrow money. We borrow when we sign mortgage papers to buy a house, when we sign finance papers for a car, when we sign a contract to make payments on furniture, or when we use a credit card to make a purchase that we can't pay off by the end of the month. With debt come consequences.

Let's start with credit card debt. Please take careful note, we're not talking about the *use* of credit cards but the *abuse* of credit cards. The credit card should be nothing more than a tool in your pocket, the same as cash or check. The basic rule of responsible credit card use is this: The first time you can't pay off the balance at the end of the month is the first month you cut up the card and close the account.

Following are some of the negative consequences we see most often. This is not an exhaustive list, but it includes the most common problems.

It produces bondage to creditors. We've already established how owing money to others creates a position of servitude. It makes people feel trapped and places them in bondage.

Credit presumes upon the future. When we borrow money, we assume that our circumstances will be the same tomorrow as they are today. Proverbs 27:1 says, "Do not boast about tomorrow, for you do not know what a day may bring forth." We are to live one day at a time. When we borrow money, we presume upon the future. We must be very careful not to get ahead of God.

Credit helps us avoid self-examination. Sometimes by borrowing money we avoid making hard choices. This isn't usually done deliberately, or even consciously, but the result is the same. Many people don't understand this reality. By borrowing, we also overlook the potential for God to redirect us through financial circumstances.

We see this all the time in talking with people about their finances. A couple places their list of debts in front of us.

"I see you have a Visa balance of $6,000. What's on it?"

"We had some emergencies."

"Well, tell us about them."

"Last week our car broke down, and it cost us $1,500 to get it fixed."

Let's stop right here. What this couple doesn't understand is this is not really an emergency. Automobile repair (and maintenance) is an expense that comes with driving a car. That expense is just as real as rent or a house payment; it just isn't due at the first of each month. But every day we drive a car, repair and maintenance expenses are heading right at us. We must plan and save for them.

What happens when we use a credit card to pay for this type of expense, though, is we evade the questions. We must ask ourselves, "Why do I borrow money for car repairs? How can I be wiser in my spending and saving so I'm prepared for this inevitable expense?"

Furthermore, we have a double hit now because not only do we need to send Visa $100 a month; we need to save another $100 a month for the next car repair.

Credit allows us to go right through God's stop sign. We do not have to wait for God—we use credit. We can "charge" ahead of Him. And it evades personal examination.

Credit cards promote impulse buying and overspending. Why do you think many retailers offer a store credit card? Studies show consumers with a credit card spend about 30 percent more than customers who pay by cash or check.

The use of credit stifles resourcefulness. To us credit in the hands of an adult is like a child sitting in front of the television; it dulls imagination, creativity, and resourcefulness.

Allow us to explain how this works in our family. Consumer credit is not an option for us. We have committed to the idea we will never owe money on a credit card, we will never have consumer debt, and we will never borrow money for a car. This also means we will probably never own a new car, but that doesn't matter to us because a car is for getting from point A to point B.

Understand, if we are ever driving a new car, we'll be smiling every day we drive it because God probably did a big miracle in our lives to allow us to pay cash. But since we know that a new car takes a drastic hit in depreciation the first few years, we would buy a car that is two or three years old.

Since we're committed to being good stewards and credit's not an option, we get creative. We ask ourselves, "Are we willing to give up something else to get that item? How can we as a family earn the money to get what we want? Is this object of our desire something God wants for us?" Not only do we become resourceful without credit, but we yield our desires to God, seeking His will and His best for us. Surprisingly, sometimes in this process of waiting on God or accumulating the required funds, we realize we didn't really want that item anyway. In other cases God provides it in a way we hadn't foreseen.

Our point is, you become more resourceful when debt is not an option. A bigger benefit is we allow God to provide for us in a supernatural way.

Credit stifles God's work in our lives. It takes away the opportunity for God to supply for us supernaturally, through a miracle. It's possible our nation stifled God from doing miracles for us because of our use of credit. The God of the Old Testament is the same God in the New Testament, and He is the same God today. He's a God of absolute miracles. But through our abuse of credit, we circumvent God's supernatural provision for us, both personally and as a nation.

Credit prevents God from using other people to accomplish His miracles for us. It's been a long time since He rained down manna. Today God tends to use people to accomplish His miracles. Let's say you and I live in the same neighborhood. Tomorrow we meet at our mailboxes. I (Dave) ask you, "How's it going, neighbor?" You reply, "Not too good. I've been out of work for three weeks. I'm $500 short for making my house payment, and I haven't got a clue where I'm going to get the money." While I'm walking back to my house, the Holy Spirit may begin prompting me. "David, you have his $500 in My checking account, at the bank." I may wrestle with God about it at first, but if I'm obedient to His prompting, I will get the money and drop it off at your door anonymously: "'When you give to the needy, do not announce it with trumpets. . . . do not let your left hand know what your right hand is doing'" (Matt. 6:2–3). That's so God gets the credit. Do you see? God has the answer; He just ran the money through my checking account over to yours. How do you think you will feel that afternoon when you find the envelope on your front porch with the money you needed? You just experienced a miracle. God uses people to carry out His miracles.

Credit makes us less available to do God's work. If you carry debt, you don't have money available to help others in their time of need as in the example above. Also, if you don't want to go to the mission field, that's simple—stay in debt, you'll never go. You may go on a short-term missions trip, but we don't know any mission agencies that will take you long-term when you're carrying debt.

We've observed instances in which God may have tapped people on the shoulder and said, "I've got a job over here in this country I want you to do." However, because of debt and the mismanagement of funds, they answer, "Well, God, I want to go, but first I have to get this financial stuff squared away, and then I'll go." Sometimes God will wait, leaving that "call" on your life. At other times, however, He seems to say, "I'm sorry, but I need it done now," and He moves on to the next person who is available and ready. Obviously, this can be very frustrating to the first person who got that call but was left behind to wade through his debt issues.

Credit causes us to spend more for purchases. The average credit card holder spends 26 percent to 33 percent more for purchases on credit than someone who pays with cash. When we use credit cards, we spend more often. We upgrade our purchases and we pay interest, thereby losing any discounts that enticed us in the first place. We know from the banking industry that the average credit card holder has thirteen cards in his pocket, and the majority of those cards are carrying a balance.

We recently reminisced about how many years in our marriage we went without any credit cards. But when I (Dave) started to travel, it became clear it's easier to travel with a credit card. I was standing in a hotel lobby with cash in my hand, but I couldn't check in because the hotel wanted a credit card imprint. I thought, *That's enough of that.* So after talking it over with Debbie, we got a credit card. But I'll admit, ever since I put that credit card in my pocket, I am tempted to buy more, more often, and to upgrade the purchase. Paying interest is not an option since we never carry a balance. We use the card only to purchase items in our monthly and yearly budget. Until we put the credit card in our pockets, however, that temptation was never there.

There's another card you carry in your pocket that causes trouble—the ATM card. Do you know what ATM stands for? Always tempting me. Now we love the convenience of ATM machines, and we each have an ATM card, but an interesting thing happened when we started budgeting. Our ATM use nearly vanished. Others who started budgeting their money experienced this also. Here's the reason: When you have a written budget or spending plan, then you are no longer reacting to life. You have preplanned your finances and spending, so your need for emergency cash at an ATM machine becomes almost nonexistent.

I (Dave) once waited behind a guy at an ATM machine. When the screen asked, "Do you want another transaction?" this guy hit the Yes button over and over. I began to wonder if there would be any money left when it was my turn. When he finally finished, he stuffed the wad of bills in his pocket, stuck his card in the other pocket, grabbed the receipt, crumpled it up, and threw it on the ground. This man's actions expressed a chaotic relationship with his money and possibly a total disregard for ordering his finances.

Our use and abuse of credit set an example for our children that may cause them real hardship in their futures. As parents, we have to be careful of the example we live in front of our children. We know our children are watching us—but we all *forget* that our children are watching us. So how we use credit and make financial decisions could either help our kids or set them up for a financial fall. We must follow God's principles of financial management, and then we must teach our children these same principles.

Let's say you're shopping with your children, and you decide to buy a new dress or a new lawn mower, and you slide that credit card across the counter, and you take that new item home. Do your children really understand that transaction? They just saw a plastic card that magically allowed you to get what you wanted. They're thinking, *Where can I get one of those cards?* Do we call our children when we're paying the bills and say, "Pals, remember when we bought [fill in the blank]_____ and took it home? Well, now I'm writing a check to pay for it. That money comes out of our bank account, where we keep the money I get paid for working." Even better, if our children see our commitment to stay debt free, the example will leave lasting influence on their own behavior.

Another reason this could be more important today than at any other time are the reports that Generation X may never make what baby boomers are making. I hope that doesn't play out, but if it does, young people will try their best to match the material and financial levels of their parents but devastate themselves financially in the attempt. They may try to match a lifestyle that was developed in a different economic time rather than during the realities of the current economy.

We must teach God's principles to our children and teenagers so when they become independent they will know how to make wise choices, along with any necessary adjustments. We want them to be prepared and available to God's call on their lives, whether in full-time ministry, missions, or a traditional career, and in whatever economic climate they face. We'll discuss this more fully in chapter 8, "Children's Bedrooms" (teaching our children about finances).

What about Consolidation Loans?

Let us share some of the most often asked questions regarding debt and credit cards. One of the first is, what about consolidation loans? Should we combine our consumer debt under one loan? This question comes up because we're trying to improve cash flow, cut payments, and secure a lower interest rate. A consolidation loan may help improve some or all of these factors, but (and this is very important!) you have to solve the problem that got you there in the first place. If you don't figure out how you got into debt and fix it, a year later you'll see new charges on your Sears, Visa, and MasterCard accounts again, and you'll still have the consolidation loan to pay off. You must solve the basic problem. If you successfully do that, then the consolidation loan may help reduce the monthly payment or interest rate.

We've worked with Larry Burkett for many years, and he sometimes recommends this: Before you get a consolidation loan, try living on a budget for six months, just to prove to yourself that you can be disciplined. If you don't learn to be disciplined, you are better off not getting the consolidation loan. Why? Because a consolidation loan will free up those lines of credit, and without discipline or focus you'll fall back into old habits and lifestyle expectations and load up on credit again—putting you in a worse situation than before.

To determine what got you into consumer debt in the first place, ask yourself:

1. Why do I use credit? Dig deep on this one. Be honest with yourself. Do you charge expensive things as a reward? Are you tempted to charge something simply because it's on sale? Do you use your credit card for "emergencies" like auto repairs or to replace appliances because you didn't set aside money earlier?

2. Do I run out of money before the end of the month? Why? People accumulate debt because they're living beyond their incomes. How can you reduce your spending; what can you give up to make ends meet? If necessary, what can you do to increase your income?

Truthfully, do you need a better-pay-
ing job or career? Does the family
need to work together as a team to
help generate additional revenue
sources?

Take time now to figure out what caused
your debt and what you can (and will) do to
improve your situation.

**PLUMB
LINE
PRINCIPLE**
*If you, O LORD, kept
a record of sins,
O Lord, who
could stand?
But with you
there is forgiveness.*
—Psalm 130:3–4a

What about Student Loans?

Some people classify student loans in a separate category
because they involve education. We don't view them that way.
Student loans are no different from other loans—you borrow
money that must be paid back. Today there's hardly any difference between the Christian campus and the secular campus; the
first place you check in is at the finance office. It's widely
accepted that you must incur a load of debt in order to get an
education. However, think about this: Many of us meet our life
partners in college. If you could start your marriage without the
burden of student loans, wouldn't you try your best to find out
how?

We believe that if we are truly committed to getting an education without going into debt, we can get that education without student loans. However, first we must purpose, decide, commit, and determine to stay out of debt. If we don't purpose to do
this, we usually take the path of least resistance: funding education through student loans. It's the path many take today. But
many don't understand the burden when the money must be
paid back and we want to buy a house, start a family, and
become involved with new activities.

Does that mean it's easier to get an education without using
student loans? Absolutely not! Frankly, it's probably ten times
harder. It may mean you have to go to junior college for two
years before you go to a university. It may mean you don't have
summers off because you're working three jobs to save up
enough money for the next year. It may mean you have to work

part-time during the college year. It means you have to spend more hours researching at the library and on the Internet for sources of scholarships and grants you can apply for. But it can be done.

We read an article about an eighteen-year-old girl who wrote about her experience. When she was a junior in high school, she found she was eligible for certain grants, so she set out to see how many student grants and scholarships she could get. Admittedly, she had a couple of unusual circumstances that qualified her for several unique opportunities, but with concentrated effort she entered college with $185,000 worth of grants and scholarships. See, if we purpose no debt, we will get creative and find other ways to fund our education. If we don't purpose it, student loans will be the path of least resistance. We can't tell you how many people we've met at seminars who testify to this principle of commitment. "But first," they tell us, "I had to determine that I would not apply for student loans. And I made it!" It's an attitude, a conscious choice, a commitment.

Why are we so adamant about this? Because we have seen what student loan debt can do to young couples.

A young lady in her mid-twenties called Dave at the office, crying and terribly stressed. Both she and her husband had attended the local university and graduated two years earlier. She was working as an administrative assistant, but her husband hadn't found work in those two years. So I (Dave) asked her about their circumstances. "How much do you have in consumer debt, on your credit cards?"

"About $8,000."

"OK. Do you also have a car loan?"

"Well, yeah, we got out of school, and we had to have a car," she said, "and everyone knows it's cheaper to drive a new car than a used car."

Her answer typifies many college grads' expectations as well as a common misbelief. The average car payment in America right now is more than $350 per month. And for $350 per month, plus the higher insurance you pay on a newer car, we can paint our car every year, we can put a new engine in our car every year, and yet we don't need to do those things every year. Many times women follow that mind-set because they don't want to deal with car affairs, and we understand, we really do, but please realize that the math doesn't support the idea that it's cheaper to drive a new car rather than a used one.

I continued with this lady. "How much do you owe on the car?"

"Twelve thousand dollars," she replied.

I took stock. This couple was in their mid-twenties with $20,000 of consumer debt. So I said, "You mentioned college. How much do you have in student loans?"

"I don't know," she said.

"Take an educated guess," I remarked, which I regretted when she started crying again. I apologized for not being more sensitive, and she answered, "About $30,000."

This couple's debt burden totaled $50,000. My heart sank. We had seen this too many times. They were most likely heading for divorce and bankruptcy. Only an extraordinary commitment—to one another *and* to get out of the deep debt they'd dug themselves into, including changing their lifestyle—would save their future together.

Here's another true story. A young couple came to see me (Dave) in the office. They had gotten married just before the young man enrolled in seminary (a pretty good reason to go to school). This guy knew without a doubt he was called to be a pastor. We spent a couple of hours together in counseling, and I also believed he was called to be a pastor. In our sessions, however, they shared how they were carrying a load of credit card debt and student loans, not to mention the additional student loans he would accumulate to finish seminary. As a result, they were experiencing some stress in their marriage over all this.

"I believe God has called you to be a pastor," I said, "but I need to share some principles with you. When you said 'I do' to your wife, you gained a new responsibility—to provide for your family. This responsibility supersedes any call to ministry. You may have interfered with God's timing when you got married, but also by the time you graduate, you'll accumulate so much debt there's not a church that can offer you a high enough salary to pay back your debts. You'll find yourself in bondage, not free to do the very thing God has called you to do. Not only that, think about the arguments that will go on behind closed doors. By the time you graduate, you may not have a wife, and that's going to take you out of any ministry you thought you were going to have."

Our discussion lasted for more than two hours, with a lot of caring concern. I finished by saying, "Don't give up on the goal; just consider all your options and pray over your priorities."

The next day the seminary student called me. "Dave, God really used you to talk to us. We realized our priorities were out of line." He took a breath and continued, "We've talked about it, and I'm going to leave school. Since I already borrowed the money for this quarter, I'll finish the quarter. When it's over, I'm leaving school so I can work, provide for my family, and pay off our consumer debt." They came in two or three more times to my office. We got them on a budget, and off they went.

Two years later he called me with an update. "Dave, my wife and I want to thank you. We paid off all our consumer debt, and I'm down to $500 left in student loans. I've saved up enough money to go back to school for a full year and graduate, and all I have to do is work part-time to get through the rest of school."

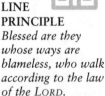

PLUMB LINE PRINCIPLE
Blessed are they whose ways are blameless, who walk according to the law of the LORD.
—*Psalm 119:1*

You see? God's going to put that guy in the pulpit, and that man will be free to do what God called him to do without the worry or burden of debt. It's all about attitude—you can choose to pursue education and God's call on your life without accumulating a burden of debt.

What about Home Loans?

In order to buy a house today, most people need a mortgage. Again, we believe this may be a consequence of where we are spiritually as a nation (back to the Deut. 28 passage from chap. 3).

You and I are caught in the consequences of a nation no longer following God. The real problem, as we see it, is not so much the mortgage; the real problem is we choose to buy houses bigger than we can afford to live in.

What's the first purchase a young couple wants to make after they get married? A house. After all, it's our God-given American right to be homeowners, isn't it? And so this young couple goes to a real estate agent and ask, "How much house can we afford?" The usual response is, "How much do you make?"

This is the couple's first major decision. Do we use the wife's income to qualify for the loan, or not? You may be surprised to know we won't say, "Don't use the wife's income to qualify." She may be very career oriented and have a good job and position. But if you choose to use the wife's income to qualify, you have one more decision to make. If God changes your circumstances or your heart, can you afford the mortgage payments on one income, or are you willing to move out of that house into a different house, or maybe out of homeownership and back to renting?

Unfortunately, most couples don't consider these possibilities. Instead, we move into our new house and say, "Oh, look what God did." Then, without warning, our circumstances change—one of us experiences a work injury, unemployment, or other major event. And isn't it amazing how during the child-rearing years, children come along? Maybe the wife wants to stay home with the new baby, but now her income is necessary to make those house payments.

Or what if God places a call on our hearts to a new ministry? God couldn't get us out of that house now. We've taken ownership of it. We've got our hands stuck to our hardwood floors, and God can't drag us out of there.because we're clutching the door frames. We will not leave this house. It's ours! So, if you choose to use your wife's income to qualify, you have another decision to make. If God changes your circumstances or your heart, will you be able to adjust to new circumstances or be willing to move out of that house?

When the question about a wife's employment comes up in counseling, we usually ask the wife, "Do you like working outside the home?" At times she says yes; she has a career. But we can't tell you how many times the wife looks over at her husband, and he's shooting visual darts at her with his eyes. Most women answer that question honestly. She says, "No, I don't want to be working. We agreed that if kids came along, I wouldn't have to work. But now I'm stuck." That's heartbreaking.

For the sake of explaining a principle, we've created the following scenario. Keep in mind, these numbers will be different depending on your specific circumstances and your geographic area.

Let's say we want a house. We meet with Mr. Real Estate Agent and give him our income amount to qualify us for a mortgage.

"OK," he says, "on that income you qualify for $1,400 a month."

We say, "Well, how much house will that buy us?"

He does some figuring and answers, "That will buy you a $175,000 house."

So now we go out and look for a $175,000 house . . . for a day or two. Then all of a sudden we're in a $185,000 neighborhood. Of course, bigger is better, and we want our kids to go to this school district and not that school district and so on. You know the scenario.

Now, here's a problem. Did you know most people can qualify for more money than they can realistically afford? If you qualified for $175,000, which you can't realistically afford, and you end up buying a house for $185,000, you're in for a rough road ahead. We also have a soul-searching question, since we've seen this before: If you qualify for $175,000, but you now apply for a $185,000 mortgage, how and where did you get that additional $10,000? Did you fudge about your income on the loan application? Did you neglect to inform the lender that Mom and Dad lent you $10,000 under the table for the down payment? If we lie or deceive anybody along the way, God is not in that purchase. If we compromise God's principles, we shouldn't try to bring God into the deal.

So you get the loan and buy the house. It's two years later. You've never missed a house payment. But now you owe Sears, Visa, and MasterCard. You never did get the yard put in or the drapes put up. You haven't been on vacation in two years. You're no longer dating your spouse. And the house isn't nearly as cute as it was two years ago.

Do you see? We don't connect these problems to buying the house because every house payment was made on time. But making those large mortgage payments stripped out all your cash flow. Your clothes and your entertainment expenses end up on your Visa card, and the bank covers your checks with overdraft protection, draining what little money you attempt to set aside. And you don't ever tie these stresses back to the largest purchase you made—the house you bought that was bigger and more expensive than you realistically could afford.

Here's what happens. Most people buy a house first and then budget around their mortgage payment, only to discover they have zero money for car repairs, zero for entertainment, zero for Christmas, and zero for gifts. But we can't (and don't) live that way. That's how they end up in debt, putting those expenses on credit cards.

Now what might happen if you do the math yourselves? Start with your *income,* and then list your living expenses. Be sure to include necessary items like insurance, car repairs, entertainment, Christmas, and gifts. In doing so, you may figure out that you can afford only $1,200 for a house payment (even though you qualify for $1,400).

Now take it to God. We believe God will bless you in one of three ways:

1. He'll say, "Not now. Stay out of the real estate market; don't worry about what your neighbors and friends are doing. I'm the owner of it all, and it's My money." That's one of the ways He'll bless you; He'll just say, "Not now."

2. Another way God may bless you is He could provide a $1,400 house for the $1,200 you can afford. He's done

a miracle for you, and you're smiling every day you live there because He stretched your dollars.

3.   God might choose to bless you by showing you a $1,200 house in a $1,200 neighborhood that you didn't even know existed, and the minute you drive down the street you know that's your house, and when you move in, you know exactly why God wants you there.

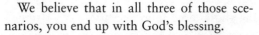

PLUMB LINE PRINCIPLE

Blessed are all who fear the LORD, who walk in his ways. You will eat the fruit of your labor; blessings and prosperity will be yours.
—Psalm 128:1–2

We believe that in all three of those scenarios, you end up with God's blessing.

The real problem is not the mortgage. The real problem is we're buying houses bigger than we can afford to live in. Please understand, we're not saying you're better off renting than owning a home. No, home-ownership is one of the greatest long-term financial benefits for most Americans. If it's God's will for your life, we hope you can be a homeowner. Keep in mind, though, that if it's not God's will for you at this time, it's not going to be any fun no matter how big or how new the house. Plus, you'll experience an enormous amount of frustration and stress.

And owning a home may not be forever. God's plans for you may include owning a house now, but later He may have something else for you to do that may require renting. As Christians, we ought to be willing to follow God wherever He leads, day by day.

In the years we've counseled others, we've learned that God may choose to accomplish His purposes in other ways, in spite of our disobedience. For instance, young couples have come to us and said, "We want to buy a house. Renting's like throwing away our money." First off, it is not their money; it's God's and He owns it all anyway. We see from their budget forms that they aren't tithing or giving any money to charities now, so maybe God directed the money through their checking account to the landlord because He knew the landlord would give it away to charities, to a church, or to others in need. God saw this couple hadn't been willing to do that themselves. So until they straighten out their priorities and put God first, they may not be able to buy a house, at least not without continuing their problems with unfaithful money management.

To sum up, debt keeps us in bondage. We must purpose to pay back what we borrow, no matter how long it takes. Bankruptcy, although an option, must be the last option. We must yield our desires to God's will. What is His plan for our lives? Where does He want to lead us? Does it involve buying a house or renting?

PLUMB LINE PRINCIPLE
Give me understanding, and I will keep your law and obey it will all my heart.
—Psalm 119:34

What about Co-signing on a Loan?

Co-signing is the assumption of another's debt by legal contract. You sign a note for somebody so they can get a loan, or somebody signs a note for you. There are problems with co-signing. First, and most important, the Bible says don't do it. Proverbs 17:18 says, "A man lacking in judgment strikes hands in pledge and puts up security for his neighbor."

If you still feel that passage gives some leeway, then we suggest reading Proverbs 22:26: "Do not be a man who strikes hands in pledge or puts up security for debts." If you have already co-signed for someone, the Bible again gives you some instructions. Proverbs 6:1–5 says, "My son, if you have put up security for your neighbor; . . . Go and humble yourself; press your plea with your neighbor! . . . Free yourself, like a gazelle from the hand of the hunter, like a bird from the snare."

Another problem with co-signing is it could be interfering with God's plan. What if God is saying, "No, not right now." God leads us by giving us money. He also leads us by withholding money. It's even possible to derail God's plans by wrongly spending the money God gave us in the first place, and then we turn to credit to get what we want, when we want it. Can you see why we must clean up our debt and develop discipline in our choices so we can get back to following God's leading through our finances?

So, if we co-sign on a loan, we could be interfering with God's plan for another person. You may argue, "Well, maybe I'm part of the answer." However, the Bible is very clear about co-signing, equating it to being hunted or being caught in a snare. It's clear that God sees co-signing as negative. In offering these cautions about it, it's also clear He prefers that we don't co-sign for someone or ask someone to co-sign for us.

Co-signing is not only negative; it also takes away God's chance to provide a miracle. God may be saying, "I know you need a second car. I am working on this couple over here—they're going to give you a car to show how much they love Me and I love you. I'm about to do it, so just be patient." Let's not circumvent God's will. After all, He's in the miracle business.

Co-signing also encourages someone to borrow beyond the ability to repay. Why do you think the lender is requiring a cosigner? Because the applicant is borrowing beyond his ability to repay.

What about our adult children asking, "Would you co-sign?" Considering Scripture, we can lovingly say, "I really want to help, but co-signing is not God's answer. There's another answer out there. Let's pray for God to reveal what it is."

But what if you didn't know God's Word on this matter and you've already co-signed on a loan? The Bible says go to your cosignee and try to make arrangements to get out of it. If that's not successful, then God expects you to honor your commitments: "Do not break your oath" (Matt. 5:33b) and "Let your 'Yes' be 'Yes,' and your 'No,' 'No'" (v. 37a). Follow through on your promise. Here's a suggested way you could talk to the parties involved: "I didn't realize I violated one of God's financial principles when we got into this arrangement. I'm here to ask for your forgiveness for not seeking what God's Word says about co-signing before we got into this loan. I promise I'll see this through to the end, but once the note is paid off, I won't be able to co-sign again." Allow the Holy Spirit to lead you in what to say.

Washing Away Debt

In this section you'll learn a way to wash away the stains of debt. We train other counselors to do this because the process works.

List your consumer debts (bank notes, car notes, credit cards, retail charge accounts, etc.) from your largest balance to your smallest. In the next column, list your payment amounts. That payment amount may be the scheduled monthly payment, an accelerated payment, or a negotiated payment. Now add up the sum of these payments to get your total monthly debt payment.

PLUMB LINE PRINCIPLE
Make it your ambition to lead a quiet life, to mind your own business and to work with your hands . . . so that your daily life may win the respect of outsiders and so that you will not be dependent on anybody.
—*1 Thessalonians 4:11–12*

For example, let's say the payments equal $440 per month. Commit to paying $440 per month to your creditors until you're out of debt. If you come up with some extra money for debts in a month (more than $440), pay the extra to the smallest balanced debt first. You're still making payments to all your creditors, but now you will focus on sending any extra money you gain to pay off those debts, starting with the smallest balance and working your way up to the largest by applying your payment amounts to the next creditor.

If you earn some extra money through working overtime, holding a garage sale, or another source and it's enough to pay off the doctor bill (your smallest balance creditor), pay the doctor bill, take the $15 you were paying on that debt and slide it up to J C Penney. Penney's was getting $25 per month, but now you will send that account $40 per month. When Penney's is paid off, take that $40 and move it up to Sears (your next smallest balance). Now Sears is getting $70 per month (the $30 you were paying plus the $40 from Penney's). Keep adding these payment amounts to the next creditor until you are paying the full $440 per month against the largest debt.

What is so exciting is that many people could be out of all consumer debt in eighteen months if they just follow this pattern. If you have large loans such as expensive auto financing, this time frame may take longer. But with a plan such as this, you can accelerate becoming free of all consumer debt.

While you're following your payoff plan, feel free to use common sense. If you have a debt with a 10 percent interest rate and another one at 18 percent, would we suggest you work on the one with the higher interest rate first? Absolutely.

Do you know why we recommend paying off the smallest debts first? Because we've seen the relief people experience when a balance is paid off. It creates momentum that helps you stay committed to paying off the rest of your debt so you can be fully free.

PLUMB LINE PRINCIPLE
Give me neither poverty nor riches, but give me only my daily bread. Otherwise, I may have too much and disown you and say, "Who is the LORD?" Or I may become poor and steal, and so dishonor the name of my God.
—Proverbs 30:8b–9

We will always remember one couple who came to us many years ago. This couple had thirty-five delinquent creditors. The husband had never had more than a $25,000 salary in his life. Their total debt was about $17,000—not a lot of money by today's standards but nearly as much as his annual salary. This couple also had six children. So we're talking a lot of creditors, a large family, and a load of debt. We helped set them up on this type of repayment plan. It took a little time to get started, but once they committed to following through, in a short amount of time they reduced their thirty-five creditors down to twenty-four creditors. They had not eliminated a lot of outstanding dollars yet, but in this couple's minds, they had come a long way. This increasing sense of relief liberated both of them, improving their relationship and spurring them on to pay off the rest of their debt load. It was hard work and it took many years, but in the process they witnessed God providing them a variety of miracles in all shapes and sizes while they eventually became debt free.

How to Accelerate a Home Mortgage Payoff

Is it possible to buy a house without a mortgage hanging over your head for thirty years or more? Yes. I'm sure you've heard of these creative ways to accelerate paying off your real estate debt:

- Paying half of your monthly mortgage payment every two weeks (equals 13 payments per year)
- Making an extra payment once a year (same idea as above but only done at one time)
- Sending a fixed additional amount each month along with your normal payment (even as small as $25 helps!)
- Paying an extra amount equal to the principle of the current month's payment (at some point the doubled principle amount may become too large to continue, but the interest saved and the years cut off the loan will be well worth the effort)

In our seminars we show another illustration, too complicated for this book, that demonstrates how we are only one generation away from paying cash for houses. Sound too good to be true? It's not! We can stop the debt cycle, even on real estate loans.

In that same illustration we introduce another challenging thought we'd like to discuss here. The longest debt term we can find in the Bible is seven years. Not thirty years, *seven* years. Today some lenders are even stretching home mortgages to forty years. We should be aware that long-term financing is a relatively recent option in our country's history, as a post-WWII product that gained momentum and acceptance from the 1940s to the 1960s.

If you calculate the cost of interest for different length mortgage loans (based on the number of years for the loan), you would be shocked at the true cost of borrowing. (See chart on the next page.)

# of Years	Principle Amount	Interest Rate	Monthly Payment	Total Interest
7	$125,000	7.0%	$1,886	$33,473
15	$125,000	7.0%	$1,123	$77,236
30	$125,000	7.0%	$831	$174,386
40	$125,000	7.0%	$776	$247,858

A majority of home mortgages are based on thirty-year terms, which in this example cost the borrower nearly $175,000 in interest over the life of that loan. Cutting the loan period in half by getting a fifteen-year mortgage (rather than a thirty-year mortgage) will reduce the total cost of interest to approximately $77,000—a savings of nearly $100,000.

PLUMB LINE PRINCIPLE
Better the little that the righteous have than the wealth of many wicked.
—Psalm 37:16

This principle also works in reverse. By *extending* the term of a mortgage to forty years, the total cost of interest increases to almost $250,000—a quarter of a million dollars—double the original principle amount ($125,000).

The numbers speak for themselves. Borrowing is expensive, and the cost of long-term financing is shocking.

Business and Debt

"But I own a business," you might say, "and I depend on a line of credit for cash flow." Here's a challenge for you: Why not make it your business plan to be your own bank someday? If you don't make that a goal, to have enough reserve funds to be your own bank, then you'll probably never reach it and free yourself from the bondage of being a borrower. You'll always be dependent upon the bank and that line of credit. If there are any bumps in the economy, such as interest rates shifting from 5 percent to 17 percent, then you've got a real problem. We've seen that happen in the past, and it knocked many businesses right out of business.

Since God "does not show favoritism" (Acts 10:34) and "causes his sun to rise on the evil and the good, and sends rain on the righteous and the unrighteous" (Matt. 5:45), His principles apply to all.

In Conclusion

PLUMB LINE PRINCIPLE

Woe to those who go to great depths to hide their plans from the LORD, who do their work in darkness and think, "Who sees us? Who will know?"
—Isaiah 29:15

To sum up, it's a decision—a commitment—to never borrow again. You have to start where you are and make that choice not to borrow from this day forward. If you don't settle this in your heart and mind now, chances are you'll always be in debt.

Next, commit to paying off your debt. If your credit cards are causing you to stumble, cut them up and close the accounts. Matthew 5:30a says, "And if your right hand causes you to sin, cut it off." Desperate times call for desperate measures, and for many people in debt, credit cards are a major stumbling block to financial freedom.

We see this all the time, when someone comes to us and says, "I really want to get out of debt. What do I have to do?"

We ask, "Do you really want to get out of debt?"

"Yes. Please, help me so I can get free of this debt and bondage."

"Get out your wallet," we say, "and give us your credit cards." At the same time one of us reaches into the drawer and pulls out the scissors.

Suddenly the person offers reasons why he can't give us his credit cards. The most common is, "But what if I have an emergency?"

We look him in the eyes and say, "How big is your God? Can He not take care of your emergencies?"

Remember, credit cards are not the real problem—it's the *abuse* of credit that is the problem—by letting balances carry over to the next month without being able to pay them off, while accumulating additional charges. When people aren't willing to give up their credit cards, we know they are not yet fully committed to getting debt free. Like Jacob in Genesis 32:24–26, they are in a wrestling match at the Jabbok River, and they will not

PLUMB LINE PRINCIPLE
But godliness with contentment is great gain.
—1 Timothy 6:6

move forward until they deal with this conflict. In Jacob's case, he got hurt in that wrestling match. But if someone who comes for help is not willing to give up his credit cards, we know the counseling session won't accomplish long-lasting results. Do we trust God, or do we just say we trust Him?

Once you've stopped the habit of borrowing or using credit, and you set up a plan to pay off your consumer debt, why not commit to paying off your real estate debt early? Start with your smallest balance debts first, though. Work your way up the list until eventually you're able to go after your mortgage debt.

Proverbs 10:22 says, "It is the blessing of the LORD that makes rich, And He adds no sorrow to it" (NASB). It is God's blessing that makes us rich. Sadly, people are trying to buy their blessings today, but sorrow is attached—debt, marital stress, rebellious children, and so on. Let's change our focus. It is the blessing of the Lord that makes us rich, and best of all, He adds no sorrow to it.

God desires only the best for us, and in His perfect will He desires that we owe no man anything except the debt of love (Rom. 13:8). We ought to keep working toward that end. Some people say, "That's nuts. You can't be totally debt free today." But see, you've already decided it can't be done, without even giving it serious and creative consideration. We generally live up to our own expectations. And what about following God's principles of finance? God will make a way if we choose to obey.

Debt is a consequence. It's a consequence of a nation not following God. We are all caught in that consequence now in this country. But we believe God's plan for us is to strive to be debt free. For most people this is a process. As the old saying goes, "The best time to plant an oak tree is twenty years ago, but the next best time is right now."

Application

What has God been talking to you about as you read this chapter?

Are you ready to make a commitment to become debt free?

What changes do you need to make?

When will you start your new plan and who will hold you accountable?

PLUMB LINE PRINCIPLE
"Because he loves me," says the LORD, "I will rescue him; I will protect him, for he acknowledges my name. He will call upon me, and I will answer him; I will be with him in trouble, I will deliver him and honor him."
—Psalm 91:14–15

CHAPTER 5

MASTER BEDROOM

Husband and Wife Financial Communication

Be subject to one another in the fear of Christ.
Wives, be subject to your own husbands,
as to the Lord. . . . Husbands, love your wives,
just as Christ also loved the church.
—EPHESIANS 5:21-22A, 25A NASB

Intimacy and communication should be at the heart of a marriage relationship, but there are inherent psychological and emotional differences between men and women that many people don't recognize. These differences create a significant impact on the way we communicate. It also impacts the way we view and use money.

It doesn't take long for a newly married couple to discover differences of opinion when it comes to money. However, they seldom take the time to stop, evaluate, and discuss those newly discovered opinions. This can grow into a very costly mistake. For a couple with many years of marriage who have never taken time to understand these conflicts, there exist layers of misunderstandings, hurts, disappointments, and a nagging sense that their relationship could be better.

Women ask, "Why doesn't my husband understand my needs in this area of our marriage? We need to get our finances in better order. Why doesn't he want to talk to me about our situation? I wish he were more involved. Doesn't he know we need a spending plan to get our finances in order? I'm so frustrated!"

Men say, "Why does my wife make such a big deal about budgets? Doesn't she realize I have other issues that are more pressing? I have to keep focused on my career and the problems at work. Why doesn't she just take care of our finances? I trust her to handle the money and make it all work."

These thoughts by husbands and wives are seldom expressed aloud. They are simply internalized and then acted out over time. By default the women end up handling the day-to-day responsibilities of bill paying and budgeting while the men blame them for any financial problems.

PLUMB LINE PRINCIPLE

You husbands . . . live with your wives in an understanding way . . . and show her honor as a fellow heir of the grace of life, so that your prayers will not be hindered.
—1 Peter 3:7 NASB

The concepts in this chapter are extremely important to the long-lasting harmony of a couple's relationship. For the two of us, understanding, acknowledging, and acting upon these unique differences and financial principles changed our whole marriage. The results were a newfound peace and happiness in our relationship and in our finances. This, in turn, flowed over into all areas of our marriage.

It really works. In our years of financial counseling, we have witnessed the strengthening of thousands of marriages when couples understood and applied the following principles.

Men: These principles work only if you are willing to work at applying them. God's Word tells us that it is the man's responsibility to demonstrate loving, caring, unselfish, protective leadership for the benefit of his family (Eph. 5:25, 28; Col. 3:19). In fact, men, if you work at these biblical principles, intimacy will grow in your marriage.

Women: If you're reading this book and your husband chooses not to, it's not fair if you look over the top of the book, smile, and say, "Honey, I've been trying to tell you this stuff for years. You should read this book! At the very least, read this one chapter. I can make a list of things we need to do." It's also not fair to leave the book lying open with sentences highlighted and double-underlined in red.

Couples: If you're reading together, don't look over at your spouse with that big "I told you so" smile. There's also no elbowing him or her, or squeezing a hand at some key paragraph!

PLUMB LINE PRINCIPLES

Therefore be careful how you walk, not as unwise men, but as wise.
—Ephesians 5:15 NASB

So then do not be foolish, but understand what the will of the Lord is.
—Ephesians 5:17 NASB

Recently separated or divorced: As you read this chapter, please consider which principles you could have better applied during your marriage. Remember, you are only responsible for your own attitudes, words, and actions. Think about which of these principles, if lovingly applied by you now, might bring healing to your relationship with your former spouse, or perhaps reconciliation. Additionally, if the principles are not addressed and corrected, they will undoubtedly carry over into future relationships.

Single: If you're single and have never been married, congratulations for learning these biblical principles now. Many married couples tell us they wished they had known or understood these principles earlier in their lives, even before they were married. It could have prevented misunderstandings, poor financial decisions, and problems during their marriages.

Marriage and the Bible

Let's look at God's design for marriage. Marriage is a covenant; it is not a contract. It is a covenant between a man, a woman, and God. And God doesn't break His covenants.

Today we live in a world of contracts. Why do we write a contract? To protect our interests in case the other party doesn't keep its part of the agreement, or if something should happen that we didn't anticipate. The truth is, contracts are based primarily on distrust. Today we write contracts for nearly everything. Is it any wonder we started thinking of marriage as a contract also?

Prenuptial agreements are contracts created in distrust. A prenuptial agreement invites the possibility in both the man's and the woman's minds that the marriage may not last. This marriage is formed without a 100 percent wholehearted commitment and is therefore vulnerable to failure. Such a marriage can't be fully fruitful or joyful for either the husband or the wife. It simply can't thrive as God intended.

PLUMB LINE PRINCIPLES

He has remembered His covenant forever.
—Psalm 105:8a
NASB

My covenant I will not violate.
—Psalm 89:34a
NASB

A marriage can't be based on distrust. To be all that God intended, a marriage between two people must be built on commitment and complete trust—a covenant. In Genesis 15, God made a covenant with Abraham over the size of his future family and heirs, and specifically the land God promised to them. Abraham prepared a sacrifice for God, and God walked in the form of a flaming torch through the middle of the sacrificed animals. Abraham stood to the side. Essentially, God said, "I am keeping this covenant."

That's the way you should see your covenant of marriage—a mutual promise of truth and trust with your spouse and your 100 percent commitment to honor this covenant no matter what happens. Unfortunately, there are legitimate cases of spousal abuse and other difficult circumstances. If you are a victim of such abuse, for your physical safety you may need to leave the house and seek shelter elsewhere. This type of damaged relationship will require godly counseling, mediation, repentance, and, hopefully, reconciliation. There are many helpful resources available that specifically address these different situations. Please note, however, that physical separation is different from breaking your covenant by divorcing your spouse.

Leaving and Cleaving

In Matthew 19:3, the Pharisees asked Jesus, "'Is it lawful for a man to divorce his wife for any reason at all?'" (NASB).

Christ's response in Matthew 19:4–6 includes a quote from Genesis 2:24: "He answered and said, 'Have you not read that He who created them from the beginning made them male and female,' and he said, 'For this reason a man shall leave his father and mother and shall cleave to his wife, and the two shall become one flesh?' Consequently they are no longer two, but one flesh. What therefore God has joined together, let no man separate."

God's plan is clear. The man must leave his father and mother and cleave to his wife. What does it mean to "cleave"? Picture holding something very precious to you very tightly with both hands.

Notice this Scripture is not addressed to the woman. The Bible says the *man* must leave his parents and cleave to his wife. This means he leaves his parents physically, emotionally, and financially. He now commits these areas of his life to his wife. This doesn't mean he and his wife can't enjoy wonderful fellowship with their in-laws. It's really a matter of his heart's focus. Does his wife come first? Unfortunately, we've talked with many wives whose husbands never really left their parents—whether physically, emotionally or financially.

Do you put your wife first?

If men truly understood this "leave and cleave" Scripture passage, they would be so far ahead of the game. Putting our wives first not only means giving them first priority by putting them ahead of our parents, but also ahead of our buddies, leisure activities, sports involvement, fantasy football, golf, and, yes, our annual hunting expeditions. In short, we are to leave our male friends and activities and cleave to our wives.

Before we lose you, we'd like to explain. When a man gives up what he wants and puts his wife first (leaves and cleaves), the long-term result is surprising. The wife will start saying things like, "Why don't you go hunting, dear?" or "Why don't you join a softball team on Thursday nights and go out and have pizza with the guys?"

When you cleave to your wife and honor her by giving of your time and attention, she is secure in your love and feels free to offer *you* freedom.

Examine your relationship with your wife right now. Has she made comments like, "Are you going to play softball again this year?" or "You're not thinking about going hunting again this year, are you?" Those are clear signals that your wife does not feel she is important in your life. You may say you love her, but your actions speak louder than any words you say.

PLUMB LINE PRINCIPLE

Do nothing from selfishness or empty conceit, but with humility of mind regard one another as more important than yourselves; do not merely look out for your own personal interests, but also for the interests of others.
—Philippians 2:3–4 NASB

Marriage Is like Adhesive

What happens when you bond two pieces of plywood together with contact cement or epoxy? Once that adhesive is set, you can't pull the two pieces apart without damaging them. Part of the plywood from one side will peel off with pieces from the other side, and vice versa. The same is true in marriage.

You can end a marriage through divorce. However, it was Moses, not God, who allowed divorce. Moses did this because of the hardness of people's hearts according to Mark 10:4–5. When you rip a marriage apart, it is never a clean break. We have counseled couples in their second marriages, and what do we end up dealing with? The first marriage. There are always emotional, financial, and personal (family) pieces still attached, causing problems and frustrations.

Marriage is a covenant, not a contract—a lifetime promise to "love and to hold, honor and cherish, in sickness and in health, for richer or poorer, until death do us part." Your marriage must be based on trust, not distrust. It's devastating to a spouse to hear the words, "If you don't get your act together, I'm out of here." This type of talk, and this kind of attitude, must be stopped immediately. We cannot offer threats if we want our marriage built on trust.

Do you need to renew your covenant with your spouse? Do you need to tell him or her, "I love you. I want to reassure you that no matter what our difficulties, I'll see them through with you to the end. We will work it out together. We are one flesh. We are a team!"

Different Responsibilities

In Ephesians 5, God provides guidelines for husbands and wives in the marriage relationship:

1. "Be subject to one another in the fear of Christ" (v. 21 NASB). Husbands and wives should be able to depend on each other for counsel, companionship, and comfort. When God created Eve, he took a rib from Adam's side, perhaps symbolic of God's intention that spouses work side by side as partners (although please note the next guideline for handling disputed matters). Interestingly, this command appears *first* in Ephesians' list of guidelines for marriage.

2. "Wives, be subject to your own husbands" (v. 22 NASB). Although husbands and wives are to work as a team, if there is an irreconcilable dispute (which should be very seldom and something which cannot be cleared up after clear, loving communication), the Bible says wives are to yield the final say to their husbands. This shows respect and honor for him. Husbands, this does *not* mean you have license to dominate, control, or coerce your wives; the Bible is very clear on how you handle this responsibility. (See v. 21 referenced above and vv. 25–37 referenced below. Also, read the section under "Left Brain versus Right Brain: Seeking the Wife's Counsel" in this chapter.) Wives, remember that God will hold your husband responsible for the decision and final outcome.

3. "Husbands, love your wives, just as Christ also loved
the church" (v. 25 NASB). Notice here that only the men
are commanded to *love* their wives; the women are commanded to respect ("be subject to") their husbands.
Nowhere in the Bible does God command the wife to
love her husband, but God does command the husband
to love his wife. Furthermore, Christ gave up His life for
the church. Men, are you willing to give up everything
for your wives?

4. "Men, leave your father and mother and cleave to your
wife" (v. 31 NASB). We discussed leaving and cleaving
at length earlier in this chapter.

For God's design for joy in marriage, each spouse must
understand and follow these God-given responsibilities.

Men, treat your wife as your partner. Listen to her counsel.
However, you are also ordained by God to be the spiritual leader
of your family. On Sunday morning *you* should be the one to
say, "All right, everybody up, let's get ready for church." It
should be you, not your wife, saying, "Let's work on our
finances together and set up a written budget." You must take
the initiative; it is your responsibility. God did not intend for
your wife to drag you along in spiritual or money matters. Men,
don't despair if you haven't done this in the past. There's no better time than now to start. You may get a little resistance from
your wife at first, but pursue her in a loving, caring, supportive
way. Deep down your wife wants you to be her knight in shin-
ing armor.

Women, respect your husband. Please don't disparage him
by your words, your tone of voice, or your attitude. You will see
in the coming sections why this is so critical to your husband
and, ultimately, your marriage.

Different Needs

Since the sixties our society has told us that men and women
are alike. Sadly, if we are told something enough times, we start

PLUMB LINE PRINCIPLE

Let your conversation be always full of grace.
—Colossians 4:6a

to accept it as truth. However, God did not create men and women alike. In addition to obvious physical differences, there are emotional and psychological differences.

It's said that men need to speak fifteen thousand to twenty-five thousand words a day, but women need to speak twenty-five thousand to fifty thousand words a day. When a man comes home at the end of the day, guess what? He's done talking! He used up all his words at work talking with clients or coworkers all day.

So when a man comes home, he may say a quick hello, sit on the couch, and read the paper. Or he turns on the television and channel surfs, driving his wife crazy. You see, he's done talking. He has spoken his fifteen thousand to twenty-five thousand words. He has no need to say anything else for the rest of the day.

Just about now the men are saying to their wives, "Hey, honey, that's exactly how I feel after a hard day at work."

However, men, true love understands that when you get home from work, your wife still has thousands of words to say to fill her quota and feel fulfilled. Love is coming home from work, leaving your day's frustrations behind you, and saying to your wife, "Honey, tell me about your day." When she starts talking, don't look over her shoulder at the television or look down and try to read the paper. Look into her eyes, smile, and listen. You are fulfilling God's command to love your wife—this time through meaningful conversation.

God Puts Opposites Together

In your marriage chances are one of you is a spender and the other is a saver. One of you likes to get up early in the morning; the other likes to sleep in late. Or one likes to stay up late; the other likes to go to bed early. One of you splashes; the other cleans up. One of you tends to forget directions and gets lost; the other one always knows where he or she is going. One of you likes to arrive early to events; the other tends to be late. One of you squeezes the toothpaste tube in the middle; the other one rolls it up neatly from the end. One of you puts the toilet paper on so it rolls from the top; the other one likes it to roll from the bottom.

God tends to put opposites together. That's by design! In our own marriage we recognize our natural tendencies could lead us into extremes. Our opposite tendencies balance each other out. God put balance in our lives by bringing us together. We've seen this in many other couples, as well.

When you wait upon God in decisions where you don't see eye to eye with your spouse, recognize the balance that's possible between you. When you finally find balance, the Holy Spirit indicates to you both, "Ah, that's where I want you." If you can't come to agreement on a matter, God's answer might be, "No, I don't want you to take this action right now." Or He may be asking you to wait.

Through our spouses God places balance in our lives. The key is to thank God for these differences instead of thinking, *Lord, why did you put this source of irritation in my life?* It is human nature to zero in on these differences as negatives rather than seeing them as a part of God's unique design for balance in our lives. Thank God for the differences.

Obviously, not all couples are opposites. However, we've observed that these couples tend to have to work a lot harder at their marriages, and a few more sparks seem to fly. What happens when you put similar sides of two magnets next to each other? They repel! If you are married to someone with a similar personality, you may find you both need to work extra hard to find a healthy balance in seeing the bigger picture, financial or otherwise.

Recognition versus Security

Now we turn to the key concept of recognition/significance versus security. These psychological needs can impact, and even shape, our individual perspectives regarding money. In our years of counseling and talking with couples, we've observed that very few people understand these contrasting financial motivations.

Typically a man's primary psychological and emotional need is recognition (or significance). A woman's primary psychological need is security. Please understand, we (men and women) need both. However, men tend to have a much higher need for recognition, and women tend to have a much higher need for security.

PLUMB LINE PRINCIPLE

As iron sharpens iron, so one man sharpens another.
—Proverbs 27:17

In everything give thanks; for this is God's will for you in Christ Jesus.
—1 Thessalonians 5:18 NASB

A man subconsciously views his job as a reflection of his abilities and a measure of his success (recognition). For the wife the house is an extension of her need for security and a reflection of her worth. If the wife works outside the home, chances are she likes the recognition that comes with her job or position. However, she is probably not working for recognition. She is probably working for security.

Once during a seminar at which I (Dave) presented this concept, a lady made a beeline toward me during the break. As an executive vice president of a large, successful company, she claimed very adamantly that I was wrong and that she was recognition oriented. However, as we talked, she evaluated her true, bottom-line motive and realized she didn't work for recognition but from a desire for security.

This is not usually so for the man. He, too, desires security, just as a woman wants and likes some recognition. However, his core need is rooted in a desire for recognition rather than security.

In the Bible, where do we usually find the men? Congregating at the city gate, talking with the other men. He's down there with the guys, talking about his latest toys or accomplishments or trying to solve the world's problems. Men tend to be very recognition oriented.

Here is another key male-female difference that affects your ability to communicate as husband and wife. Women tend to be very relationship oriented while men tend to be very goal oriented. Women want to talk about a problem—carefully discussing all the details. Men want to get to the bottom line, solve it, and move on to the next issue—with the minimum number of words or details as possible.

Here's a very real illustration from our own marriage. We homeschool our children, a wonderful choice but still subject to the normal ups and downs of life. When I (Dave) arrive home from work, I can usually tell whether it's been a good day or not—the general mood hangs in the air and seems to radiate through the front door.

One day had been a particularly stressful one for Debbie. I sat with her on the couch, looked into her eyes, and lovingly asked, "Debbie, tell me about today. What caused so many problems and frustrations?" Sounds like a pretty caring approach, doesn't it? Like, I'm scoring big points as the perfect husband.

Debbie described her day for about ten minutes, giving me the details. When she finished, I responded, "Well, if you had simply done this, this, and this, none of that would have happened."

You guessed it—this was not a right response! Any points I thought I'd scored with Debbie vanished. Fortunately for me, Debbie recognized I was being 100 percent male; take in the facts, solve the problem, and move on to the next matter. She patiently looked at me and said, "David, I don't want a solution. I know the solution. I just want you to sympathize with me and the fact that I had a rough day."

Another example of relationship orientation (female) versus goal orientation (male) came up on our vacation during a leisurely breakfast with Dave's brother and his wife at his country club. We enjoyed our meal overlooking the first tee and ninth green. The conversation drifted to why women couldn't play the course before noon on Saturdays.

Dave's sister-in-law exclaimed, "I've never understood that rule. The women here play golf just as well as the men."

Dave's brother agreed but compared how men and women approach golf. He explained, "When a foursome of men tee off, they take turns hitting the ball and then head for their ball with a few short, friendly exchanges." The male mind-set is focused on the objective: *I've got to get that ball in the hole.* (He's goal oriented!)

"However," he continued, "when four women tee off, they comment on each shot. Then the four women walk together to the first person's ball, usually talking on the way, and then watch her hit the next shot. Then they walk together to the second person's ball, usually talking on the way, and watch her hit. Then they go to the next person's ball, and so on."

Do you see? The women are having a meaningful relationship. They are relationship oriented. Not the men. Men are goal oriented.

What does your husband want to do when your family sets out on a vacation, driving in the car? Get there! Men will drive ten thousand miles in one day, nonstop. Along the way the children start chorusing, "Daddy, we have to go to the bathroom." Dad answers, "Thirty more miles, we can make it thirty more miles. Everybody hold on and don't talk." Men have to conquer the driving to the vacation destination and get there fast, so they can unpack and conquer that necessary hindrance, so they can then get to the golf course and conquer that challenge.

What does the wife say as the husband speeds nonstop down the freeway? "Honey, why don't we pull over at the next rest stop and get out of the car for awhile? The children can play, and we can have a nice picnic lunch." What is she really saying? "Let's quit being goal oriented and have a meaningful relationship with each other."

Many women don't realize that in a man's mind, this is the Indianapolis 500. He spends three hours passing every car, jockeying for position, and getting the car into the perfect spot. Then when the wife wants to pull off the freeway at the rest stop, he watches all those cars go by that he just spent three hours passing.

When a husband gets frustrated, women, please understand it's not personal. It's simply because he feels the interference with his efforts to conquer. And, men, please realize that your wife is not trying to frustrate you. She simply wants to enjoy the journey and the people she loves. Remember, she's relationship oriented.

These male-female tendencies are evident even at a young age. One Sunday morning we decided to take separate vehicles to church because I (Dave) needed to do something right after the service and the rest of the family wanted to head directly home. The three boys hopped in my extended-cab pickup truck with me. Debbie climbed into the van.

Instantly, the boys urged me, "Dad, get out of the driveway first! Don't let Mom get ahead of you. You have to beat her to church!" Imagine the rising testosterone level in the truck!

I let Debbie pull out of the driveway ahead of us but not because I was being chivalrous. As a male, I wanted to make sure Debbie had a fair chance, so I gave her a head start.

All during the twelve minutes of driving time to church, the boys yelled, "Dad, get in front of her! Pass her now, Dad, pass her now!"

"Boys, I can't pass her. It's a solid double yellow line on the road."

"It doesn't matter, Dad," they exclaimed. "You have to beat her to church!"

Minutes later we pulled into the church parking lot right behind Debbie. The boys threw open the truck door, jumped out, ran to Debbie, and announced, "Oh, Mom, you won!"

Calmly, Debbie asked, "Won what? What are you talking about?"

"You won the race!"

"There was no race," she said.

I leaned over toward Debbie, looked her squarely in the eyes, and said, "You don't understand. It *is* a race!"

Men, Women, and Emotions

Another male-female difference to understand in order to improve communication in your marriage is this: Men tend to separate their emotions from the thought process, sometimes to the great frustration of women. For women, thoughts and emotions tend to be tied together.

For example, why is it that many men like to hunt, whereas most women do not? It's all about conquering, it's goal oriented, there are no emotions involved, and there's absolutely no talking allowed. It's all male stuff! To the man he's simply going hunting—sometimes for sport but usually to provide food for the family. However, the woman is thinking, *You're going to shoot Bambi's daddy?*

But there's a downside to this male tendency to separate emotions from the thought process. You may have heard this cry from a woman: "I don't understand why my husband just walked out on our family. Maybe I can understand how he could walk out on me, but how could he walk out on the children?" Men can more easily separate their emotions from the thought process, making such a devastating choice. It is much harder for a woman to separate her thoughts from her emotions.

A Word Picture of Recognition versus Security Orientation

Recognition versus security is probably the greatest factor when it comes to marriage and financial matters. This difference in how men and women view money becomes so obvious in a counseling session. We'd like to offer further explanation through a word picture.

Imagine your marriage as a boat. It can be a big, beautiful, twin-engine yacht, or it can be a long, sleek, fast sailboat. You decide. Right now your boat is tied up at the dock getting ready to set sail on your marriage voyage.

What is the husband doing? He's waving at his friends on the dock, saying, "Hey, guys, check out the boat. Pretty nice, huh?" Remember, he's recognition oriented. The guys on the dock (his friends and business associates) are looking on with admiration and saying, "Nice boat! I'll bet that thing really goes fast. What kind of engine does it have? How much horsepower does it generate? What features did you get? You sure picked some great colors. Looks fantastic!"

The husband is getting all his strokes and encouragement (recognition) from his friends and coworkers. He's deeply involved with his career. The people at work and all his friends like him. He's climbing the corporate ladder. He is going to hold an important position in the company some day. He is recognition oriented.

Is the wife waving at all her friends on the dock too? Is she saying, "Hey, girls, check out the boat?" No. She is looking around, examining everything. She is asking, "Is this boat going to float? Do we have a first aid kit? Are there enough provisions for the trip? Do we have extra sails or a repair kit? Do we have money set aside in case we get stranded?" You see, she's security oriented.

The problem? We aren't aware of these differences when we get married. Then we set sail on our marriage voyage. We calmly cruise along the shoreline where we can still be seen. The husband waves at his friends along the shore. He's smiling and thinking, *Life is wonderful. My career is going great. I'm due for another promotion.* His friends and business associates are calling out, "The boat looks great. It sure cruises along nicely. Way to go!"

Suddenly we hit a financial swell in the water, and the boat rocks a little. Both the husband and wife glance around and say, "Whoa, what was that?"

What is the first thing the wife says when you hit a financial swell? She reaches for the helm. She says, "Let me take care of the checking account and handle the finances." What's happening? She is grabbing for the helm of her life—financial security. She feels if she handles the money, she can protect that important part of her married life. Being security oriented, she certainly doesn't want the finances out of control. She also sees her husband is focused on his career rather than the finances.

Now, women, please understand; men will shuck any responsibility you want to take over for us. When the wife says, "Let me handle the finances," men quickly agree. While he's waving to important people on the shore, he says, "Thanks, honey. You take over the checking account. I have to concentrate on my career, friends, and reputation down at work. I can't be bothered with our monthly finances."

Men usually don't have a clue that the wife is security oriented. He assumes she is just like him. In turn, the wife doesn't understand her husband's need for recognition; she assumes he is just like her. However, she starts to wonder why he isn't more involved or concerned about their money issues. Usually, none of this is intentional or deliberate. It simply happens by default and a lack of understanding.

At this point the wife picks up the responsibilities for the finances. She handles the checking account and pays the bills. We are again sailing along in our marriage with this new financial structure of responsibility. The wife can see that their expenses are greater than their income. However, she doesn't want to bother her husband with the problem because of his attitude or past financial arguments, or she hopes she can get it all worked out at some point. Her intentions are good, but neither she nor her husband is dealing in reality or truth.

A little while later, after a couple more years of marriage, we hit a much bigger financial wave that really rattles our boat. The husband and wife quickly raise their heads from their responsibilities and look around. Again they ask, "Whoa, what just broadsided us? What's going on?"

At this point in the marriage, the husband now sternly says, "Hey, I give you all the money. What's going on here? Why are we having these problems? Why aren't you making our finances work correctly and covering all the bills?" Understand, the budget has never balanced, even from the start of the marriage. The husband freely charges family entertainment expenses and large-ticket items that he feels are rewards for his hard work, and the wife has been afraid to seriously address the shortfall she knows exists.

Right about now the wife is holding onto the helm for dear life. The husband can be totally oblivious to the fact that her world is coming apart. That's because he's focused on work, maybe even church and friends. Remember, he's recognition oriented, not security oriented.

Men, this is why it's so important that you be involved with the finances. Your wife is security oriented. Loving her is to understand and acknowledge this difference. You don't have to be the bookkeeper, but she needs you to be involved.

Here's the good news. You could be in thirty-foot financial swells with waves cracking over the top of your boat, but that's not the end of the world for your wife. What is important to your wife is that you, her husband, get involved and help take over the responsibilities at the financial helm. Now, men, when you grab hold of the helm, don't push your wife off the boat. You need her and her God-given gifts.

It's been our observation that if a husband will lovingly take hold of the helm, a wife can ride out five years of disciplined living as long as she knows her husband has hold of the helm. However, men, if at some point you let go of the helm, chances are her knees will buckle, and she will reach over and grab for the helm again. Remember, she is security oriented, and it is very important to her to know that the financial helm is secure and that the two of you are headed in the right direction.

It's so important for a man to understand this need in his wife for security. Again, this doesn't mean he has to do the books. He just needs to be involved in the process. Whoever is the better bookkeeper should probably be the one to do the books. The exception to this is when the couple is in serious financial trouble involving creditors. Then we feel the husband must take responsibility for their financial situation and protect his wife from having to talk to or negotiate with their creditors. Additionally, the husband must remain 100 percent honest about their situation and keep in close communication with his wife.

Also, wives, please understand your husband is recognition oriented. You're not going to change that reality in him. Furthermore, he will not be able to change his natural need for recognition just because he now understands your need for security.

Over the years we've seen the damage inflicted on a spouse through the critical words or glances of the other spouse. It's so important to guard your tongue and your attitude. If you resent your spouse for your financial problems, you will probably demonstrate your feelings through critical words, looks, comments, or actions. The attacked spouse will start backing up emotionally, and if the attacks continue, he or she may withdraw completely to the point of leaving the relationship.

PLUMB LINE PRINCIPLE
Let all bitterness and wrath and anger and clamor and slander be put away from you, along with all malice. Be kind to one another, tender-hearted, forgiving each other, just as God in Christ also has forgiven you.
—Ephesians 4:31–32 NASB

Our hope is that you clearly see this difference in your individual needs: the man's need for recognition and the woman's need for security. Be aware, it can be reversed for some couples, so keep that in mind. However, do you see why about 95 percent of all the calls for financial counseling come from the wife?

Knowing these differences, husbands and wives need to accept each other and remember that men and women approach life and money from different viewpoints. To do so will bring peace, harmony, and happiness to the marriage.

We Speak in Two Different Languages

Because you and your spouse speak the same language, it's easy to assume you are communicating. Wrong!

Sometimes we would be better off if, when we first got married, one spouse spoke French and the other spoke Spanish. Chances are we would get more communicating done because we'd accommodate each other in trying to understand each other. However, because we both use the same words, we think we mean the same things. But that's not always true. Men and women use the same words but often mean different things. Understanding this concept will help you in your communication, including your financial discussions.

For example, one year Debbie and I attended a weeklong seminar in downtown Seattle. We had been at this event nearly all week, and our children had spent the last two days with another family. We hadn't seen them at all those last two days.

We had arranged to pick up our children on the final evening of the conference at a water park near our home.

Leaving the conference that last day, I (Dave) wondered aloud whether we should leave Seattle and cross Lake Washington by driving across the Interstate 90 bridge or the Evergreen Point Floating Bridge. Debbie replied, "I–90 is faster."

Now, to a male like me, the statement "I-90 is faster" was nothing more than a mathematical equation. It didn't even enter my thought process that Debbie's response might have any other meaning. It was simply an equation easily solved by running the numbers.

So I ran the numbers. The drive across either bridge would take approximately twenty minutes. It was 6:15 P.M., and we were supposed to pick up our children at 7:00 P.M. That gave us forty-five minutes to make a twenty-minute drive.

Well, I love driving across the Evergreen Point Floating Bridge on a beautiful summer, Seattle night. When I reached the interstate, which way do you think I headed? You guessed it; I turned north toward the Evergreen Point Floating Bridge. A few minutes later on the bridge, all cars came to an unexpected halt. An accident ahead blocked traffic.

Within seconds I could tell Debbie was upset. Her body language was loud and clear: *We are going to be stuck on this bridge for the next hour. We're not going to reach the water park by seven o'clock. The park closes at seven! They will turn out the lights and close the gates. The family who has been caring for our children needs to get home. Our kids are going to be left standing alone at the gate with the lights turned out, the gate closed, wearing nothing but their bathing suits, with wet hair, holding damp towels and crying, "Where's Mommy and Daddy?"* Do you get the picture? Debbie was a little uptight about this situation.

It got worse. I made a slight tactical error at this point—I laughed! The reason I laughed was because I realized that back in downtown Seattle, we were talking two different languages. Debbie's actual words were, "I-90 is faster." However, that was not all Debbie said with those three simple words. Debbie actually said, "I haven't seen my children for almost a week. I miss my children. I want to get to them just as fast as we can so I can love them, hug them, and spend time with them. David, if you can get this car across that lake without bridges, I really want you to do it!"

My male brain didn't hear any of those hidden words. When I told Debbie why I laughed, she understood and wasn't quite as upset with me. (We made it to the water park on time, thank goodness!)

Remember, men and women speak in two different languages. At times I will ask, "What's the matter, Deb?" She will respond with a short cold, "Nothing." So I simply reply, "Oh, good, I'll go do the yard work." She clearly said, "Nothing." However, is that really what she said in that one word? Definitely not. What she really said was, "David, pursue me. Something is the matter and please keep talking with me until we get to the problem."

Here is another killer exchange. I say, "What's the matter, Deb?" She responds with a quick, ear-piercing, "You know!" Women, please understand, we males usually haven't got a clue as to what is wrong! That is why we asked you the question.

Sometimes women think men are real deep, real serious thinkers. The truth is that men have a hard time reading between the lines. Many times their thoughts are completely on the surface. What you see is what you get.

Because men and women talk two different languages, husbands and wives need to work at saying what they really mean and making sure they understand what is really being said.

Tips on Communicating

Men, ask your wife clarifying questions or repeat back what you think she said. Say to your wife, "I really want to make sure I understand." Then repeat what you thought she said, in your own words. You might be surprised to hear, "No, dear, that is not what I'm saying at all. This is what I'm saying."

Wives, you have a part in this process also. Do the best you can to say what you really mean. Remember, sometimes men can have a difficult time reading between the lines.

Left Brain versus Right Brain: Seeking the Wife's Counsel

Let us demonstrate another male-female difference that can be a big factor in couples' communication and the making of wise financial decisions.

It is said that the left side of the brain is the logical side of the brain, the side that thinks in order, sequentially. The right side of the brain is the creative and emotional side of the brain and where verbal communication originates.

Statistics indicate that men tend to be left-brained and women tend to be right-brained. We're convinced that men conduct these studies, and they are so left-brained that anything less looks right-brained to them because we believe that women use much more of both sides of their brain than men do. Today there is medical and scientific knowledge to prove that point.

A man's brain tends to work like an old-time adding machine. Punch in the number, pull the handle, punch in the number, pull the handle, punch in the number, pull the handle, hit the total button, and out comes an answer. He thinks in sequential, chronological order.

A woman's brain functions more like a preprogrammed computer. Data goes in from all different sources and out comes an answer. Guess what the woman sometimes says? "I don't know how I came up with that answer."

What does that do to the man's left brain? It sends it into fry! Actually, after the man hears his wife say, "I don't know how I got that answer," what does he do with her conclusions or her counsel? He dismisses them as irrational and throws them out. Because she can't explain how she came up with that answer, his left brain determines her conclusions are not logical and are therefore invalid.

We've observed this played out in many different scenarios. A man comes home and proclaims excitedly to his wife, "Honey, I have us a winner. We will make big bucks on this one! Our ship has come in!" After the husband explains the bullet points (and maybe one or two details if she's lucky), the wife shrugs her shoulders, wiggles her head, and says very cautiously, "I don't know. I just don't have a good feeling about this."

The man instantly bristles. "Feelings? What do feelings have to do with this deal? Look, here are the facts. This is a sure winner!"

She again responds with a lot of uncertain body language and says, "I don't know. It just doesn't feel right to me."

Men, when your wife says she doesn't have a good feeling about something, pay serious attention. She may not be able to explain her conclusion, but believe it, she's processed the information and something doesn't quite add up. Or she senses something she can't quite explain. A woman's intuition is a God-given gift.

When a woman says, "I don't have a good feeling about this," God may be prompting her. Pay attention. God might even be telling her, "Would you please talk to your husband? He's about to lose all My money again, and he quit listening to Me a long time ago."

We know several successful couples who understand the importance of this God-given gift called woman's intuition. These husbands do not make any major decisions in their businesses without their wives' involvement.

Here's how they take advantage of this gift. One business-man calls a meeting, perhaps a dinner or lunch meeting for all parties involved. He includes his business associates and their wives. During the meal they discuss all the details as well as make small talk.

After the meeting each of his business associates asks his wife privately, "How do you feel about this matter?" These wives may be able to give complete, technical counsel because they understand the business. However, the husbands also want to know how their wives "feel" about the deal.

If she indicates thumbs-up, that doesn't mean throw all caution to the wind. It simply means she feels all right about it at this point. If she indicates thumbs-down, it doesn't mean it's a dead deal. It simply means to slow down, something is wrong somewhere, or something may be going on behind the scene that has not completely surfaced yet.

Let us share what may have just happened at that lunch or dinner meeting. Let's say I invite Debbie to such a meeting to meet all the players in a pending transaction.

We walk into the meeting and approach the key person involved. I say, "Debbie, I would like you to meet Bill. Bill, I'd like you to meet Debbie." Bill sticks out his hand to Debbie to shake it. In a split second Bill's eyes go zoom-zoom (up and down). He just scanned her body with his eyes.

Debbie picks that up (usually subconsciously) and thinks, *This man just scanned me with his eyes. This man does not have moral freedom in his life. If this man does not have moral freedom in his life, then God is probably going to have to chastise this man at some point. If God chastises this man and I have gone into a partnership or serious transaction with him, then I'm going to get chastised along with him. I'm security oriented and I don't want to get chastised, especially financially. Therefore, I don't have a good feeling about this deal.* This exchange and thought process all happened in a split second, in the twinkling of an eye.

Or Bill sticks out his hand to Debbie, and for a split second, his eyes go to the right or the left. He can't look her square in the eyes or keep good eye contact. Debbie notices and thinks, *This guy seems to be hiding something, or he may be dishonest in some way.* I personally believe Debbie goes through the same thought process as before. Many times it works its way right back to the security factor, and she comes to the conclusion, "I don't have a good feeling about this deal."

We have seen this in counseling. A self-employed couple will be in our office. Their business is failing or has already failed. After talking for awhile, one of us asks the wife, "What was your counsel to your husband about starting this business?" We can't tell you the number of times that the wife glances at her husband, then looks back at us, and says, "I told him not to start this business. I never felt good about it from the beginning. I tried to tell him my concerns, but he just wouldn't listen. He shrugged me off and told me he would work out all the details. As his wife, I finally gave in and signed the loan papers to start the business. I wish I had not given in because now our situation is worse than before we started the business."

PLUMB LINE PRINCIPLE
Be subject to one another in the fear of Christ.
—Ephesians 5:21 NASB

Men, your number-one source for counsel—after the Word of God—is your spouse. It is not your business associates or your friends. It is your spouse. This is also true for the wives. Men must seek the counsel of their wives, and, wives, you ought also to seek the counsel of your husbands.

It is critically important that your counsel is godly and biblical. In Genesis, Sarah advised Abraham to use the culturally accepted practice of impregnating her handmaiden to fulfill God's promise of giving them a son (using a human solution rather than waiting for God to fulfill His promise). The result was the births, story, and problems of Ishmael and Isaac. That decision has brought untold anguish to the Middle East, as Ishmael's descendants (the Arabs and Palestinians) war against the descendants of Isaac (the Jews). It's imperative that we seek God's wisdom when offering counsel to our spouses.

When There's a Problem . . .

In our own marriage we use the words "I feel" to help explain some problem or emotion we're experiencing. One of us will say, "Right now, I feel like this (feeling explained)." Or, "I feel like you are doing this to me (action explained)." We have learned that "I feel" does not mean it's absolute truth, but it conveys how one of us feels about an issue or attitude. The feeling is based upon the information, data, and emotional input the person has at this time. Using "I feel" allows us to express our concerns without sounding judgmental or critical. For instance, I (Debbie) may feel hurt about something. It was never Dave's intention to hurt me, but right now I feel hurt. So I tell Dave how I feel. This helps us be totally honest with each other and gets those little or big hurts on the table. We can then acknowledge the hurts and work our way through them, before they take root and blossom into bitterness, withdrawal, or negative reactions.

A Calming Disclaimer

Our statements about male/female tendencies are general in nature. We know some people can be exact opposites of how we present these relationship tendencies. We encourage you to see if you identify with what you've read and glean whatever fits your circumstance and marriage. The key is to zero in on the truth related to your specific issues and marriage.

Summary

What are the key mistakes couples tend to make?

- Leadership: The husband avoids leadership in the area of finances. He's not willing to be actively involved in the finances. He, in fact, leaves all the responsibility for the family and household to his wife.
- Teamwork: One or both spouses are not working as a team. One partner in the marriage dominates the finances and budgeting, the wife holds onto the finances too tightly, or the husband uses money to control his wife.
- Priorities: Priorities slip out of line. Wives put their children ahead of their husbands. Husbands put their careers or activities ahead of their wives and children.
- Needs: Partners may show insensitivity to the spouse's needs—the wife's need for security and the husband's need for recognition. The husband should say, "Honey, let's make time to put together a working budget and

tracking system. Let's set some short-term and long-term goals together." Wives should say, "I am so thankful for you. I appreciate your hard work to support this family. You are a hard worker and good provider."

• Time: Husbands and wives must spend time with their spouses in order to maintain a healthy marriage. Make time to discuss issues and work through problems. Also, keep a regular "date night." Spend quality one-on-one time with each other, without the children. Make plans to go over your finances on a regular basis, such as weekly or monthly.

How Are You Doing?

If we want a thriving, vibrant, and satisfying marriage, we need to know how our relationship is going with our spouse. Guess who has a finger on the pulse of a marriage? The one who is relationship oriented—the wife! A wife also needs to know that her husband is concerned about their marriage relationship and that he is intimately involved in making it a success. Gary Smalley endorses using a scale of one to ten as a great way to find out how you are doing in your marriage, so here's how we do it.

I lead Debbie to a quiet, peaceful setting and ask, "Debbie, on a scale of one to ten, where's our marriage right now?"

Debbie has to answer with a number. She might say, "Dave, right now, I feel like we are at a six." Chances are my initial emotion will depend on where I thought we were on the scale. I might have thought we were at an eight or a four. So I might feel lifted up or let down, depending on what I had expected to hear.

At this point I've learned not to say, "What will it take to get us to a ten?" It's too difficult for us to get from a six to a ten. So instead I ask, "Debbie, what will it take to get us to a seven?"

Then Debbie tells me the number-one thing she wants me to work on in the marriage. She doesn't give me a list: just one thing. Men tend to be able to work on one issue at a time, unlike women who can deal with many issues at once. Chuck and Barb

Snyder, two longtime ministry friends, cover this topic well in their books and seminars. I recognize this fact: Give me one item at a time, and I can try to conquer it and move to the next one.

Now, wives, please don't answer your husbands with a cold, flippant statement such as, "Just get your life together! You're a mess!" You must communicate something specific your husband can work on. Remember, we're trying to increase communication and work on improving the relationship.

And, men, let me share two things with you from the bottom of my heart. The first time I asked Debbie to rate our marriage on a scale of one to ten, we had been married for sixteen years. I was more nervous than when I proposed to her. I did it, so I know you can do it! Also, if you ask the follow-up question ("What will it take to get us to the next level?"), in my experience it's going to be one thousand times simpler than what you thought your wife would answer.

When Debbie told me what she wanted me to work on that first time I asked her, it was so easy to accomplish. Furthermore, I would have never thought of it. But once I heard what Debbie wanted, it was easy to accommodate her.

Another benefit is if you ask the question and work on that one thing she tells you, you will go right past seven on the scale and head up to an eight or nine. She sees you as loving, caring, and concerned. She sees you trying to work on the marriage and the issue she brought to your attention. If you're sincere in your effort, you will score big points, even if you don't always succeed. If you drop the ball, simply ask for forgiveness and start working on it again.

Be aware that you could be at an eight one month and then a five the next time you ask. This is an ongoing, every-day process, but it's absolutely a great way for a husband and wife to communicate!

This technique may be used by the wife asking the questions of the husband, but we believe it truly works best when the husband takes the lead by asking the questions. Remember, the Bible tells the husband to cleave to his wife, and God gave him the responsibility for leadership in the family.

**PLUMB
LINE
PRINCIPLE**

*To sum up, . . . be
harmonious, sympa-
thetic, brotherly, kind-
hearted, and humble
in spirit; not returning
evil for evil or insult
for insult, but giving
a blessing instead.*
—1 Peter 3:8–9a
NASB

Application

What has God been talking to you about
as you read this chapter?

What can you do to make your marriage
healthier, happier, and more successful?

What changes do you need to make to
improve your marriage?

For what do you need to take responsibility and ask forgiveness of your spouse?

What commitments do you need to renew?

When will you take your wife out and ask her the one-ten
question?

If you have never been married, how can you become better
prepared for a future spouse?

CHAPTER 6

Dining Room

Charitable Giving, Tithes, and Offerings

"When you give a banquet,
invite the poor, the crippled, the lame, the blind,
and you will be blessed."
—LUKE 14:13-14A

L et's head over to the dining room, where we entertain, share our food and fellowship, meet people's needs, and offer hospitality. This room perfectly represents our financial giving and charitable contributions. For Christians this includes tithes and offerings.

First, we feel it's important to define the word *tithe* because it's often used as a generic term in the church today to mean "donation" or "giving." However, *tithe* is not a generic word. It literally means "tenth" or "10 percent." It doesn't mean 3 percent; it doesn't mean 8 percent—the word means 10 percent. In our years of teaching seminars and counseling, we've talked with many people who thought they were tithing, but, in fact, they were simply giving—not tithing.

Why do we give? We don't give to get closer to God. We give as a result of being closer to God. Giving is simply an outward tangible indicator of our inner spiritual commitment. We give in reverence to God because He is God. This is a kind of Old

Testament giving. New Testament giving could be called "grace giving." We give because of God's grace for us. He saved us from eternal separation from Him through the free gift of His son, Jesus Christ. So we give in response to a God who would do that for us.

How much should we give? It would have been easier if Jesus, Paul, Peter, and other New Testament writers had plainly stated, "Thus says the Lord, all Christians should give 10 percent of all income they receive." They didn't, so we need to look at all that is recorded in the Bible about giving. In the dining room, we'd like to give an overview of what the Bible says about giving, including how we should pay our pastors.

"Moses Math"?

One of the most often-asked questions about tithing (giving 10 percent) involves beliefs about Old Testament Law versus New Testament grace. Some say, "Tithing was part of the Old Testament Law, but now we're under a new covenant, a covenant of grace. Therefore, tithing no longer applies."

To study this issue, I (Dave) asked a few Christian counselors to join me. We went through all the biblical passages about giving and tithing and about Law and grace. We were amazed at what we discovered. Every reference for the New Testament Gentile Christian was about *sacrificial* giving—going *beyond* the Law. Christ dealt with this same argument about grace versus law. In effect, He told his listeners, "You don't like the Law. Well, the Law says don't commit murder, but I tell you, do not hate. The Law says don't commit adultery. I say, do not lust. The Law says tithe, and you obey. But see the widow giving her last two coins? I'm telling you, give sacrificially."

Again, giving money is the outward evidence of an inward spiritual commitment. We give as a result of being closer to God.

In Genesis 14, Abraham gave a tenth of the spoils of war to the high priest Melchizedek. This was unusual because he did this four hundred years before the Mosaic Law was written— tithing preceded the Law. How did Abraham know to give a tithe to the high priest? It's our personal belief that Abraham knew to give a tithe of the spoils of war because God probably had a conversation long before with Adam and Eve in the Garden of Eden about giving. How did their sons Cain and Abel know to bring an offering (Gen. 4:3–5)? We believe that the God who created us also created in us the need to give, because giving is an outward demonstration of our spiritual relationship with Him. In addition, we are created in the image of God, and God is a giver: "'For God so loved the world that He *gave*'" (John 3:16a, emphasis added).

PLUMB LINE PRINCIPLE

Keep your lives free from the love of money and be content with what you have, because God has said, "Never will I leave you; never will I forsake you."
—Hebrews 13:5

What Jesus Said about Tithing

Some say, "Jesus didn't talk about tithing in the New Testament." Let's take a look at Matthew 23:23: "'Woe to you, teachers of the law and Pharisees, you hypocrites! You give a tenth of your spices—mint, dill and cummin. But you have neglected the more important matters of the law—justice, mercy and faithfulness. *You should have practiced the latter, without neglecting the former*'" (emphasis added).

The Pharisees were obviously diligent about tithing. They tithed everything, not only their income but even their spices. However, Christ saw the attitude of their hearts. He berated them for neglecting "the more important matters"—justice and mercy and faithfulness—while Jesus concluded, "These are the things you should have done without neglecting the other" (the tithe). So Christ encouraged deeper heart attitudes even while affirming the practice of tithing.

Why should we give and why the emphasis on 10 percent? We touched on this briefly, but we would like to answer this in more detail. In the Old Testament, Deuteronomy 14:22–23 says, "Be sure to set aside a tenth of all that your fields produce each

PLUMB LINE PRINCIPLE
The crucible for silver and the furnace for gold, but the Lord tests the heart.
—Proverbs 17:3

year . . . so that you may learn to revere the LORD your God." We give in order to show reverence for God and who He is. He is God almighty, the Creator of the heavens and the earth.

In the New Testament, 2 Corinthians 8:1–3 says: "And now, brothers, we want you to know about the grace that God has given the Macedonian churches. Out of the most severe trial, their overflowing joy and their extreme poverty welled up in rich generosity. For I testify that they gave as much as they were able, and even beyond their ability."

Did you notice that in the Old Testament we read about giving a tenth, and in the New Testament we read about giving generously? So how much should we give? Biblically, the minimum is the tithe, which is 10 percent. For the Christian, this is not a goal but a starting place. This means we should make it a goal to give much more than 10 percent.

There was no mystery to the Old Testament Jews about tithes and offerings. Some passages suggest the Jews gave an average of 23 1/3 percent every year. Scripture indicates they had two tithes every year and a third tithe every third year. The first of these tithes went to the priests and Levites; the second went to the widows and orphans. The third tithe they were allowed to consume during a special festival at which "fellowship sacrifices" (also known as "peace offerings") were offered. Similar to a large potluck supper, this festival was attended by everyone—the priests, all family members, and the poor. As for New Testament Christians, Paul wrote that those in Macedonia "gave as much as they were able, and even beyond their ability" (2 Cor. 8:3). Generosity was the standard in the New Testament church when it came to giving.

Malachi 3:8 says, "Will a man rob God? Yet you are robbing Me! But you say, 'How have we robbed You?' In tithes and offerings" (NASB). As we've already established, the tithe is 10 percent, so offerings are above and beyond the tithe. The minimum, or the starting point, is 10 percent. Anything above that amount can be considered an offering, each of us giving "as we are able."

Blessings and Consequences of Tithing

This passage tells us there are consequences attached whether we withhold the tithe or give it: "'You are cursed with a curse, for you are robbing Me, the whole nation of you! Bring the whole tithe into the storehouse, so that there may be food in My house, and test Me now in this,' says the LORD of hosts, 'if I will not open for you the windows of heaven and pour out for you a blessing until it overflows'" (Mal. 3:9–10 NASB).

God said, "And test Me now in this." This is the only place in the Bible God says, "Test Me." That's what He said. "Put Me to the test. You have to make the first move, and then I can respond."

We'd like to be very candid here. The first time we read this passage many years ago, both our left brains (especially Dave's) started working overtime. "This is not going to work, Lord. Look at the math!" But God's Word said, "Test me now in this." So we agreed that we wanted to act in obedience and give God the full 10 percent.

When we wrote that first check for 10 percent, we prayed: *Lord, we don't understand how we'll make it, but like You said, we're putting You to the test.* Ever since that day we have been overwhelmed by God's provision. Our needs have always been met and without using debt. If you obey God in tithing, it doesn't mean there won't be lean times, and it doesn't mean there won't be prosperous times. But the Bible says, "'Test Me now in this,' says the LORD of hosts, 'if I will not open for you the windows of heaven and pour out for you a blessing until it overflows'" (Mal. 3:10).

Here's an interesting observation; we rarely hear tithers complain about tithing. Only nontithers complain about tithing. We believe it's because tithers know why they tithe. They take God at His word, they acknowledge His ownership of all their resources, and they are grateful for His love and provision. Plus, tithers understand the blessings that come with obedience.

Malachi 3:11 says, "'Then I will rebuke the devourer for you, so that it will not destroy the fruits of the ground; nor will your vine in the field cast its grapes,' says the LORD of hosts" (NASB).

To "cast its grapes" means to drop them off the vine; and "the devourer" destroys the fruit—or in practical terms, we don't get to use the money or possession, or it becomes of no value. It is almost as if God is saying, "All right, here's the deal: I want you to tithe, although I will never force you to give it because it's a reflection of where your heart is with Me. However, if you give Me the tithe, I'll rebuke the devourer; I'll keep the enemy out of your finances. If you choose not to give it to Me, the devourer will come."

PLUMB LINE PRINCIPLE
Now he who supplies seed to the sower and bread for food will also . . . enlarge the harvest of your righteousness. You will be made rich in every way so that you can be generous on every occasion, and through us your generosity will result in thanksgiving to God.
—2 Corinthians 9:10–11

What most people don't realize is this principle is at work in everyone's finances. In other words, everybody "tithes," it's just a matter of where the money goes. Is it given to God's work and multiplied? Or is it devoured? If you don't give to God, you will see the money devoured—your car breaks down more often, you're spending more on medical bills, and so on, until it's gone. It's devoured. When we're talking with a couple who used to tithe but who later quit for whatever reason and we show them this passage of Scripture, it's like a light comes on. They say, "When we tithed, our money always went further." This is God's economy.

Net or Gross?

This is another question we're often asked. "Should we give 10 percent based on our net income or gross income?" We like to answer (tongue in cheek, of course), "Well, do you want a gross blessing or a net blessing?"

When we wrote that first tithe check, it was for 10 percent of our net. As we studied more about tithing in the Bible, we realized that many passages talked about giving from the increase or from *all* of our income:

- "Be sure to set aside a tenth of all that your fields produce each year" (Deut. 14:22).
- "Honor the Lord with your wealth, and with the first-fruits of all your crops" (Prov. 3:9).

When we tithed on the net amount, but paid taxes on the gross, in effect we elevated the government to a position higher than God. That's when we decided that if we're going to test God as He said in Malachi 3:10, let's test Him all the way. At that point we moved up to tithing on the gross amount.

A reassuring word to the self-employed here. Usually, a business will tithe on its gross *profit,* not gross *revenues.* Some businesses don't even work on a 10 percent margin and could tithe themselves right out of business! However, we have met business owners who work off large margins and choose to tithe on their gross receipts.

Where Should We Give?

The Bible says, "Bring the whole tithe into the storehouse, so that there may be food in My house" (Mal. 3:10 NASB). The storehouse had specific purposes, including feeding the priests and Levites (Num. 18:24–29), and feeding the Hebrew widows, orphans, and the poor (Deut. 14:28–29). In today's context we believe our tithe should go to the local church since many of its functions are similar to the storehouse.

As for offerings, this category of giving is above the tithe amount and can be directed to other ministries, missionaries, and biblical causes that God lays on your heart. For us, it doesn't matter if the cause is tax deductible. When we see a need that we feel God wants us to meet, we give money to it. Giving without focusing on what we get out of it is how we believe God wants His people to operate.

What if you don't like what your church is doing? We encourage you not to withhold your giving. Instead, make an appointment with the pastor and elders and bring up your concerns. Be sure to back up your claims with Scripture. Then if they say, "We don't care," chances are you're sitting in the wrong church. Hopefully, they will consider your comments, and everyone will grow from the experience.

PLUMB LINE PRINCIPLE

For you were called to freedom, brothers; only don't use this freedom as an opportunity for the flesh, but serve one another through love.
—Galatians 5:13 HCSB

Giving to Others

How should you handle it when an individual in financial trouble comes to you with a request for money? There are several Scriptures to consider.

- "Give to the one who asks you, and do not turn away from the one who wants to borrow from you" (Matt. 5:42).
- "'Give to everyone who asks you' . . . Do to others as you would have them to do you" (Luke 6:30–31).
- "He who is kind to the poor lends to the LORD, and he will reward him for what he has done" (Prov. 19:17).
- "Share with God's people who are in need. Practice hospitality" (Rom. 12:13).
- "Then Peter said, 'Silver or gold I do not have, but what I have I give you'" (Acts 3:6a).
- "If a man shuts his ears to the cry of the poor, he too will cry out and not be answered" (Prov. 21:13).
- "One man gives freely, yet gains even more; another withholds unduly, but comes to poverty. A generous man will prosper; he who refreshes others will himself be refreshed" (Prov. 11:24–25).

God's principles always offer balance. Here are some cautions:

- "If a man will not work, he shall not eat" (2 Thess. 3:10b).
- "The laborer's appetite works for him; his hunger drives him on" (Prov. 16:26).
- "A sluggard does not plow in season; so at harvest time he looks but finds nothing" (Prov. 20:4).
- "All hard work brings a profit, but mere talk leads only to poverty" (Prov. 14:23).
- "He who works his land will have abundant food, but he who chases fantasies lacks judgment" (Prov. 12:11).
- "Do not throw your pearls before swine" (Matt. 7:6a, NASB).

You can see these Scriptures endorse being generous with the needy but also declare that poverty comes to the lazy or to those who lack judgment. There's a difference between someone who is in need through no fault of his own and someone who gets into financial trouble as a result of his own irresponsibility. God wants us to use discernment in our giving when we are approached with a need.

If someone gets injured or loses their job, we can feed the person or offer a monetary gift to alleviate the immediate need. Or, like Peter, if we don't have extra money at the moment of crises, we can offer our time or service—run errands, help with chores or child care, or even spend time in prayer with that person. However, if the person in need is not looking for work or proves to have a chronic pattern of trouble, the individual may need to suffer the consequences of his own behavior. We're talking about love and compassion balanced by wisdom and discernment.

That's why churches could benefit from a financial ministry to assist in discerning these situations. We've been involved in many cases as a third-party counsel. For instance, when a young adult runs into financial trouble, the parents usually offer to stand by their adult child financially as long as he or she has repented and added accountability. A church with a financial ministry can help in that way.

This raises another point. An important source that is usually overlooked when someone is in need is the family. In 1 Timothy 5:8 we read: "If anyone does not provide for his relatives, and especially for his immediate family, he has denied the faith and is worse than an unbeliever." Family is God's first line of defense.

Many people think the church or government should meet people's needs, but according to this Scripture, we ought to ask our family members first: parents, siblings, aunts, uncles. Unfortunately, today we hear, "My parents got divorced five years ago, and they ended up bankrupt. I don't talk to my brothers and my sisters, since we don't get along. And I don't even know where my aunts and my uncles are." So the church is bearing the burden of families falling apart attempting to meet needs in people's lives that perhaps should have been met by family members.

God's first line of defense is family. If you find yourself in financial need, we suggest you go to a family member and ask for help from that person first. If he says no, then ask your church. If someone comes to *you* with a need, tell him you want to help but ask if there's anyone in the family he could approach first (talk with him about this Scripture about the family helping). And if someone in *your* family comes to you with a legitimate need, be prepared to help, as long as he's doing what he can to improve his situation (use discernment so you don't end up protecting him from consequences and maturity).

Another area we ought to support with our money involves those who minister to us spiritually. If somebody ministers to us spiritually, we should minister back financially. Paul describes this principle in his letter to the church at Corinth: "Who serves as a soldier at his own expense? Who plants a vineyard and does not eat of its grapes? . . . For it is written in the Law of Moses, 'Do not muzzle the ox while it is treading out the grain.' Is it about oxen that God is concerned? Surely he says this for us, doesn't He? . . . If we have sown spiritual seed among you, is it too much if we reap a material harvest from you?" (1 Cor. 9:7–11).

Barnabas Ministry, of which we are employees, is supported by people just like you, as other parachurch organizations are supported. If you receive benefit from a ministry, support that ministry so it can continue in its work, and even help it grow to minister to many others.

We are also to help our Christian brothers and sisters. First John 3:17 says, "If anyone has material possessions and sees his brother in need but has no pity on him, how can the love of God be in him?" God says that if we're not taking care of each other's needs in the Christian community, how can the love of God be in us?

We also need to take care of those who are unbelievers. Matthew 5:42 says, "Give to the one who asks you, and do not turn away from the one who wants to borrow from you." In context, this verse is talking about unbelievers, and God says we should meet their needs as well (using discernment).

Sometimes we are busy talking about the gospel to unsaved neighbors, friends, or relatives, but we are insensitive to their needs. What would happen if, instead, we met their needs first in a meaningful way, without obligation? Then they may be driven to ask, "Why would you do this for me?" We can answer, "Oh, let me tell you about Jesus Christ and what He's done for me."

In summary, how do you decide whom to support? Support your local church, those in need, those who are ministering to you, family members, and other worthwhile causes God lays on your heart. Choose with care to ensure good stewardship of the money you contribute to others.

What If God's People Tithed (Gave 10 percent)?

Back to Malachi 3, verse 12: "'All the nations will call you blessed, for you shall be a delightful land,' says the LORD of hosts." Are nations calling the Christian community blessed today? No. But this verse says all the nations will call you blessed.

Here's what is happening in church giving today. Per capita giving by church members has been in a decline and is now at about 2.5 percent of income. The minimum God talks about is 10 percent. What if giving went up to 10 percent as God's Word indicates? Most church budgets would be three to five times larger than today.

Statistically, this would raise an additional *$78 billion dollars*. Analysis of UNICEF information by EmptyTomb.org estimates that the world poverty need is about *$80 billion*. With a potential of $78 billion in the Christian community, we could, by tithing, wipe out world poverty.[1] All we have to do is obey God in giving our tithe.

And that's not even counting the offerings above the tithe. If we all gave 10 percent and followed God's direction in offerings, we could send missionaries into the world fully funded. Yet every day missionaries go to the fields half funded and right into financial bondage. Then we wonder why they burn out or why some who return are depressed and even angry at God.

If we gave as God tells us to, we'd be feeding the hungry and clothing the naked. We'd be taking care of the single parents lined up at our doors, dying financially. In addition, if your church wanted to build a building and God's people were obedient in giving their 10 percent, the church could delay building for a year or two while it maintained its ministry budget and then build with cash and no debt. One of the reasons churches across the nation are borrowing money today is because God's people are not following God's financial principles, including tithing and sacrificial giving.

This level of giving is not impossible. In the aftermath of September 11, 2001, charitable contributions reached $456 million.[2] We are a generous nation. Now we need to be obedient to God.

Imagine, if we Christians obeyed God in our giving and if our churches followed God's principles of finance in not borrowing, the unsaved world would be curious as to how we do it and be drawn to the people of God by their generosity. As it is, one of the gods the world serves is money. So unbelievers look at our struggling churches and say, "Why would I want your God? He's broke. Plus, you only want me for *my* money." Instead, if they see the church growing and the members helping others both inside and outside the church, unbelievers will be drawn to see why and may begin to desire the same God we serve.

PLUMB LINE PRINCIPLE

Be rich in good deeds, and . . . be generous and willing to share. In this way [you] will lay up treasure for [your]selves . . . so that [you] may take hold of the life that is truly life.
—1 Timothy 6:18–19

Other Tips on Giving

Other biblical passages offer practical guidance on giving. First Corinthians 16:2a says, "On the first day of every week, each one of you should set aside a sum of money in keeping with his income." This passage supports regular giving. Setting aside a sum of money in keeping with one's income is proportionate giving—giving a percentage of income (not a dollar amount). We could pray, *Lord, as I view your plan for my life this year, I believe you want me to give this percent of everything that crosses my path.* Let's give regularly and proportionately.

We are also to give of our firstfruits. In Exodus 23:19, God says, "Bring the best of the firstfruits of your soil to the house of the LORD your God." Remember, the Hebrew nation was an agrarian economy, so the Lord explained this in farming terms. It's like they could pray, *Lord, thank You for the increase. I planted the seed, I weeded it, I watered it, but I didn't have one thing to do with the crop growing. You did that. I joyfully give back to You the first and best portion of the increase in acknowledgement that You are the Creator and Owner of it all.*

That's what the tithe represents; it represents the whole. *Thank You, Lord, for what You provided and for this increase.* What does that mean for us today? Our tithe should be the first check we write, not the last check. *Thank You, Lord, for this paycheck. Thank You for this job You provided. I now give back to You the best, the first 10 percent of the money.*

That's firstfruit giving. When you find yourself writing a check in church, examine your heart. Are you giving the first-fruits of your income? Did you come with giving in mind, or was it a last-minute decision? For some people, it's part of their worship and ritual to write a check in church for their tithe. However, if we were really honest, it would be revealed that many people are giving God seconds, thirds, fourths, and leftovers. The first and best belongs to God. Give of your firstfruits.

What if I'm in Debt?

This is a complicated, emotional question. Some financial advisers say you ought to tithe (give 10 percent) even when you're in debt. We don't disagree but also offer slightly different advice.

We've worked with people dealing with truly desperate situations with enormous debt. First, we look at Scripture together, and they recognize how they got into trouble. Many times they're ready to acknowledge God's role as owner and their role as stewards, and they want to tithe to show their obedience to God. We encourage them to pray about their situation. The Bible says, "You do not have because you do not ask" (James 4:2b NASB).

If you're in a similar situation, you need to understand how you got into debt. Was it because of a problem with priorities or a lack of knowledge or both? Acknowledge that God is owner of it all and that you are God's steward of His resources. He wants you to manage what He's given you.

We advise that after you pray for God's direction, you might consider taking a step of faith. You could start giving God a portion of your income, out of each paycheck. We urge you also to make an appointment with the leaders of your church to explain your situation. Make clear that your goal is to increase your giving while paying off your debt. Make yourself accountable to them for this plan, and ask them to pray for you. Sometimes unexpected miracles happen. "Therefore confess your sins to each other and pray for each other so that you may be healed. The prayer of a righteous man is powerful and effective" (James 5:16). "Do not be anxious about anything, but in everything, by prayer and petition, with thanksgiving, present your requests to God. And the peace of God, which transcends all understanding, will guard your hearts and your minds in Christ Jesus" (Phil. 4:6–7).

By doing this, you align yourself under godly authority, your church leaders have a chance to be involved in the process, and you are all working toward the day when you are free to give as you desire and as God leads. However, God may make clear that He wants you to give the full 10 percent now, so be willing to make way for God to do a miracle for you.

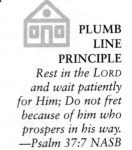

PLUMB LINE PRINCIPLE
Rest in the LORD and wait patiently for Him; Do not fret because of him who prospers in his way.
—Psalm 37:7 NASB

There is a balance we must keep in mind. When we borrow money, we've promised to pay our creditors a certain monthly payment. God requires us to keep our word. That's why this topic is complicated and emotional.

What if My Spouse Doesn't Want to Tithe?

About 99.9 percent of the time, we're asked this question by wives, so let's address this question from the wives' point of view first and then the husbands'.

To wives: If your husband doesn't want to tithe, the Bible says the wife should be subject to her husband (Eph. 5:22a), and we believe that supercedes the call to giving. Wives, please understand that if you're in this difficult position, God knows your heart. He will hold your husband accountable for the tithe, not you.

This is not to say you should *assume* your husband doesn't want to tithe. God said, "Test Me on this," so go to your husband and say, "Honey, I've been reading the Bible and learning about tithing. I feel we should be giving 10 percent from our income. What do you think?" If he's against it, perhaps try offering this suggestion, "We could test God. Would you be willing to start by giving 3 percent? We could give 3 percent for six months, and if we're worse off at the end of six months, I'll back off. If we're the same or better, let's increase it. Let's take God at His Word."

To husbands: If your wife is not a believer or is struggling with giving, this gets a little more complicated since God gives you the responsibility of leadership in your family. However, realize that the Lord cares more about your wife's soul than a tithe, so if it becomes a stumbling block, consider suspending your tithe temporarily while you love your wife to the Lord. Perhaps you could also try the same method suggested above, by asking your wife to "test God" and agree to tithe 3 percent at first for six months and increasing the amount to 10 percent if your financial situation later is the same or improved. Remember, she is security oriented and may just want assurance you're handling the other 90 percent responsibly before she can emotionally release the 10 percent.

What about the Cheerful Giver Passage?

"Each man should give what he has decided in his heart to give, not reluctantly or under compulsion, for God loves a cheerful giver" (2 Cor. 9:7). Usually we hear, "The Bible says we should give what we decide to give, and that we shouldn't give if we're not cheerful. God loves a cheerful giver." However, most people misunderstand the context of this verse. Paul was talking about a prior commitment by the Corinthians. Earlier in this passage he said, "I came to town a few years ago, and you said you were going to take care of this church responsibility. I am now sending Titus to collect on what you promised." See, the Corinthians had already decided in their hearts what they would give a couple of years earlier, and he was holding them to what they promised. When we make a commitment to God in our giving, we shouldn't second-guess ourselves or our commitment. Give eagerly, not reluctantly, with cheerfulness and thanksgiving.

Sacrificial Giving

We should also strive to give sacrificially (beyond our tithe and offerings). In Luke 21:1–4, Jesus described the sacrificial gift from a widow: "As he looked up, Jesus saw the rich putting their gifts into the temple treasury. He also saw a poor widow put in two very small copper coins. 'I tell you the truth,' he said, 'this poor widow has put in more than all the others. All these people gave their gifts out of their wealth; but she out of her poverty put in all she had to live on.'" Notice, the Lord honored her by recording her sacrificial gift for all eternity. You and I can learn to give sacrificially as an outpouring of our love for God. It's not easy, because it's a sacrifice.

For Pastors (and Church Members Who Pay Them)

One topic that we get questions about and that comes up regularly within the Christian community is, How much should we pay our pastor? Since this chapter discusses our giving of tithes and offerings in our personal finances, it's appropriate to address this question.

Church leaders call us and ask, "We are reviewing our pastor's salary package. Do you have any national figures or averages we can use as a guideline?"

We usually respond, "Rather than using national figures, we encourage church leaders to look to the local community, find out what professionals make in your area, and double it. That's how much we should consider paying our pastors." Of course, the caller is usually quite stunned.

The Bible says, "The elders who rule well are to be considered worthy of double honor, especially those who work hard at preaching and teaching" (1 Tim. 5:17 NASB). We are also instructed not to "muzzle the ox while it is treading out the grain," (v. 18) indicating the oxen should be allowed to eat the grain even as they work. Furthermore, the Bible says a "laborer is worthy of his wages" (v. 18). God is clear about paying wages, and paying them well, to those who serve us in ministry.

The Bible gives a reason why this is so important: "But if anyone does not provide for his own, and especially for those of his household, he has denied the faith and is worse than an unbeliever" (1 Tim. 5:8 NASB).

Our pastors are people, too, and they must provide for their families. This includes the same living expenses we all face. Just as married couples and singles need to plan and budget, keep up with the cost of living, and raise children, so do our pastors.

If you can't trust your pastor and his spouse to figure out what it costs to fund their family's needs (which includes insurances, car repairs and replacement, education, vacation, entertainment, gifts, and retirement) and then present the truth to the church leadership, why is it that you trust them to impart the insights and truths of the Word of God?

If a pastor discloses an amount of money for his budgeted family needs, we as a congregation need to fund it for them. Understand, when we talk about the pastor telling the leadership of the church the family's financial needs, we're not talking about a congregational meeting. We're talking about disclosing this information to a small, intimate, discrete committee of church leadership (i.e., the personnel committee) that will then advise the leadership of the church regarding the amount of pastoral salary the church needs to fund and the raises needed from one year to the next.

We have regularly counseled with pastors, sometimes sent to us by their own church leadership. After reviewing the pastor's finances, we've contacted the church. "You need to give your pastor a raise," we've advised. "You're not paying your pastor enough money to live in the very community you called him to minister in."

Churches don't do this intentionally. It's simply a process of misguided steps that happen over time. In courting a new prospective pastor, churches rarely talk openly about personal finances. The leaders usually don't ask the candidate to submit a projected budget for his family in this new position, much less request a financial statement (including a list of debts, credit report, etc.).

Sometimes the pastor hasn't been using a written budget, he doesn't really know his family's total financial needs, and he hasn't spent adequate time researching the cost of living in the area where he's interviewing.

If the leadership and the pastor follow these steps prior to the offer and acceptance of a call, our churches, pastors, their marriages, and families would be happier and healthier. If we were willing to deal in complete truth before the call is made by the church leadership or the position accepted by the pastor and his family, the leadership could say, "We really like you, but this church cannot pay what you need for your family. That is more important than your coming to our church as pastor. God will lead us to the right minister and you to the right church." Or if the church really wants to hire this pastor, then it will raise the money to fund the pastor's family budget needs before calling him to the position.

Furthermore, if the pastor knows his family's budgeted needs, he can honestly tell the church leadership, "You know, I really like your church. It has been wonderful getting to know you. However, the salary you offered will not meet my family's needs, and that is more important than my coming to your church. God will lead me to the right position and you to the right person. Please pray for me, and I will pray for you."

Unfortunately, these honest, forthright conversations rarely take place. The church doesn't know the pastor's full financial situation, or the pastor doesn't know his family's full budget and salary needs or the true cost of living in this new area. So what typically happens is the pastor accepts the call to a new church (along with the agreed-upon salary). Then, usually within a month or two of paychecks, reality sets in that it's not working. This is the same for anyone who accepts a job position for a salary below the family's basic needs. It won't work over the long haul. Eventually debt surfaces along with other stresses.

To complicate matters further, pastors rarely have someone in whom they can confide. They can't tell anyone that their family is struggling financially. They are expected to be perfect and not make mistakes. When they begin floundering, they sometimes use credit to buffer the shortages, which begins a slow slide toward bigger problems: financial bondage, discontentment, bitterness (especially by the wife), rebellious children, with all these troubles rippling outward, creating church discord and more. They may even start looking for another church to pastor.

Another experience we've seen in counseling is when someone in the church who sells real estate as a vocation offers to help the new pastor locate and finance a house. Just as was discussed in the laundry room (debt chapter), the pastor ends up buying a house that's more expensive than his family can truly afford. Again, this is not intentional; it's simply both parties not understanding or dealing with complete financial truth. However, this good-intentioned transaction may end up more complicated because of the dynamics within the church, particularly if the real estate person is a church leader.

Please don't misunderstand—many churches do a wonderful job compensating their pastoral staffs. However, for the majority of cases that we've been involved in as counselors, the pastor was underpaid. Often the problem can be traced back to the interviewing and hiring process, with unintentional mistakes made by everyone involved. Let's work together with our church leadership to ensure that we're properly paying our pastors, communicating clearly with the pastoral staff, and always dealing with the truth in love.

In Summary

When it comes to finances, we should deal in truthfulness and love. When it comes to giving, tithing is an attitude of the heart. We need to give in acknowledgement of God's ownership of it all. Be willing to test God in your giving. Put God first, and He'll take care of you. Learn to give with a cheerful heart. And give of your firstfruits, give regularly, give proportionately, and learn to give sacrificially. We pray that you will know and experience God's blessings in this area of giving.

Application

What has God been talking to you about as you read this chapter?

What changes do you need to make in the percentage you give, when you give, and how you give?

What worthwhile organizations is God prompting you to help with your time, talents, and money?

Do you need to seek financial counseling from someone in your church?

PLUMB LINE PRINCIPLE

Give, and it will be given to you. A good measure, pressed down, shaken together and running over, will be poured into your lap. For with the measure you use, it will be measured to you.
—Luke 6:38

CHAPTER 7

KITCHEN

A Recipe for Financial Freedom (Planning and Budgeting)

> Commit to the LORD whatever you do,
> and your plans will succeed.
> —PROVERBS 16:3

Now it's time to prepare God's recipe for financial freedom. This menu has the fat-free, low-calorie, low-sodium, high-fiber ingredients for optimum financial health. If you're serious about living life unburdened by debt, stress, and strain, then this chapter is for you.

Statistics indicate that an overwhelming majority of the population have no written proactive plan for their finances. Most Americans deposit their paychecks into their checking accounts and then react to life, hoping someday for financial independence and prosperity. But as the saying goes, "Those who fail to plan, plan to fail."

The following list[1] reveals why being better managers of our money is so important:

- Seventy percent of Americans are living paycheck to paycheck (Source: *Wall Street Journal*).

- Less than 30 percent use a written monthly budget to manage household finances.
- Ninety-five percent [of American couples] argue about money-related topics on a regular basis.
- Less than 10 percent have computed a target goal for retirement.
- Sixty-two percent will retire with less than $10,000 income per year (source: U.S. Census Bureau).

In addition, out of approximately 104 million households in America, about 40 million households earn more than $50,000 per year (40 percent). Of these, 11 million earn more than $100,000 per year. However, only 4 million households have a net worth of $1 million or more, and the typical American household has a net worth of less than $15,000.[2]

If you're like most Americans, you don't have a plan, but you need one. If the word *budget* makes you cringe, call it your cash-flow management plan instead. The fact is, a written budget helps you get control over the money you're responsible for managing. Getting control and keeping control will let you achieve the freedom you crave for your future.

Luke 14:28 says, "For which of you, wanting to build a tower, doesn't first sit down and calculate the cost, to see if he has enough to complete it?" (HCSB). God says, figure out the cost. A budget reveals the truth of where we are, and where we want to go. "You will know the truth, and the truth will set you free" (John 8:32 HCSB).

Sometimes it hurts to see the truth, but that's the start of the process that sets us free. Where do you need to go? And what steps do you need to take to get there? Here is a lasting, biblical recipe for financial freedom—it's simple and easy to prepare:

1. Start with a large measure of prayer.
   - "But you, when you pray, go into your inner room, close your door and pray to your Father who is in secret, and your Father who sees what is done in secret will reward you" (Matt. 6:6 NASB).
   - "Pray without ceasing" (1 Thess. 5:17 NASB).

2. Pour in the factual ingredients.
   - "For which one of you, wanting to build a tower, doesn't first sit down and calculate the cost, to see if he has enough to complete it?" (Luke 14:28 HCSB).
   - "The plans of the diligent lead surely to advantage, But everyone who is hasty comes surely to poverty" (Prov. 21:5 NASB).
   - What is your net spendable income? This is what you have left after tithes, offerings, and taxes.
   - What does it cost you to live? What are your *actual* monthly expenses, including seasonal, irregular, and annual expenses?

3. Add strategic planning.
   - "Commit to the LORD whatever you do, and your plans will succeed" (Prov. 16:3).
   - "The mind of man plans his way, But the LORD directs his steps" (Prov. 16:9 NASB).
   - "But the noble man devises noble plans; And by noble plans he stands" (Isa. 32:8 NASB).
   - What are your future goals?
   - What changes do you need to make to meet these goals?
   - Specify how you will cut expenses and/or increase income.

4. Mix together with discipline.
   - "He who ignores discipline comes to poverty and shame, but whoever heeds correction is honored" (Prov. 13:18).
   - "No discipline seems enjoyable at the time, but painful. Later on, however, it yields the fruit of peace and righteousness to those who have been trained by it" (Heb. 12:11 HCSB).
   - Start tracking your income and expenses.
   - Start saying, "No" or "I'll have to wait."
   - Commit to no more consumer debt.

5. Give it time.
   - "The seed which fell among the thorns, these are the ones who have heard, and as they go on their way they are choked with worries and riches and pleasures of this life, and bring no fruit to maturity" (Luke 8:14 NASB).
   - "Let us not lose heart in doing good, for in due time we will reap if we do not grow weary" (Gal. 6:9 NASB).

The Recipe in More Detail

After the first step (prayer), go to step 2 of the recipe: List your income and expenses. Figure your net spendable income, the total after tithes, offerings, and taxes. This is the amount available for spending and for which you need to set up a plan to manage.

Next determine the amount of your current spending. What are your actual expenses? This is important, because if you set up a budget without checking your actual costs, it may set you up for failure. What we've seen happen is a family thinks they're spending $400 dollars a month for food, so they start a budget with $400 in that category. However, if they look back in their checkbook for the past three months, they might discover they really spent $550 per month. So when they try to live on their guess of $400 a month and then exceed their budget before the end of the month, they say, "Oh, budgeting doesn't work. Let's just quit." The problem wasn't the budget—it was starting with an inaccurate and unrealistic number for the family's food and household expenses.

Therefore, figure out your actual spending to give you a factual starting point (we'll get to cutting expenses later). The more factual history you consider, the more realistic your starting figures will be. Also, don't forget those annual bills, such as car insurance, registration tabs, renter's or homeowner's insurance, property taxes (if you pay them directly to the county), life insurance, vacation, and sports and entertainment. Add up these annual totals and divide each by twelve months to get your monthly expense total.

Step 3 of the recipe requires strategic planning to establish your goals. What do you see as your future needs? For most families, an important priority will be to pay off debt. You should also set aside a monthly amount for reserves, to cover annual bills, auto maintenance and repair, and emergencies. You will want to save for gifts (birthdays, Christmas) and later, a vacation. To meet these goals, you need a control system. There are software programs like Money Matters Deluxe (from Crown Financial Ministries), Quicken, Microsoft Money, and others. Or you could keep track of your monthly budget and spending in a simple spreadsheet or even in a notebook. The important thing is to keep it simple and make it work for you.

When couples write down their income and expenses in a counseling situation, they are revealing the truth about their finances. In some cases this shows they cannot realistically afford the house they're living in, cannot afford the payments on that new truck, or perhaps the most painful, cannot really afford to keep their children enrolled in Christian school without making major changes. These revelations usually bring tears. When a couple realizes they may need to sell their house for a place they can afford, the wife feels vulnerable because she's security oriented. Or when they realize they may need to sell that pickup truck, the husband feels vulnerable because he's recognition oriented. Or when they realize they need to pray about taking their kids out of Christian school, they are both in tears because this involves a point of conviction. But the facts become clear on paper—their income cannot support their level of spending, and credit has become a way of life with increasing balances carried forward month after month.

Another typical scenario is the husband and wife who ask for counseling and who already figured they are $200 a month short. However, as we list their actual expenses, we learn they planned "zero" for entertainment, "zero" for car repairs, and "zero" for gifts. We explain this is not realistic and that these are the same expenses people typically end up charging on credit. When we finish making the list—this time identifying all expenses—they can see they are actually $400 a month short. Before this exercise the husband and wife had felt like there was a heavy fog covering their marriage; they knew something was wrong, but they couldn't identify what. Completing a realistic list of expenses cut through the fog. They could clearly see they'd been overspending by $400 a month.

PLUMB LINE PRINCIPLE
Come near to God and he will come near to you. . . . Humble yourselves before the Lord, and he will lift you up.
—James 4:8, 10

Two things happen at this point. First, this couple now has a specific prayer item. Before doing this exercise, they had been praying, "Lord, we need more money." A prayer like that is too vague, and God doesn't generally get the glory when He answers. However, now they can pray, "Lord, we need $400 a month. Please show us how to cut our expenses by $400 a month or how to raise our income by $400 a month or maybe a combination of both."

Second, this is now a defined goal. It's not an unknown amount of money; it's $400. Solve the $400 problem, and you probably just found financial freedom. The truth is, if your life depended on it, you could figure out in the next thirty days how to generate $400 a month. It all comes down to setting priorities and committing to them.

There is an interesting phenomenon when an individual or a family has a monthly shortfall. In many cases the amount the individual or family is short each month is usually very close to their total monthly consumer debt payments. This means if the person or family pays off their debt, they could live within their means without additional income. They just have to solve the problem they've created (debt), which will take creativity, commitment, and time while they get their financial house in order.

Let's examine one more element. In the scenario described above, it's very typical a family like this may earn $3,000 per month and give $100 to their church or a charity. If they say it is their heart's desire to tithe, then we suggest they increase their amount of giving to equal a tenth of their income ($300). Remember, God said, "Test Me in this" (Mal. 3:10). So we add $200 to the amount of their giving category. This increases their shortfall from $400 to $600 a month. Now we pray for this new goal and act upon it. If we can solve $400, with a little extra effort we can solve $600. Solve the $600 shortfall, and this family is living within their means, and they're tithing too. By embracing the truth of their situation and accepting their role as stewards rather than owners, they begin to experience freedom even as they prepare a plan to get out of debt and better manage the money God entrusted to them. By including the full tithe now, they don't underestimate what it will take to get back on track financially and have peace in their giving.

If you have this type of monthly shortfall and you're married, it's easy to consider having your wife work outside the home. Before you make this decision, however, please figure out her net income to make sure you aren't actually losing money. We counseled a married couple who both worked outside the home. Even though the wife worked full-time, they continued to have a monthly shortfall. Her gross income was about $1,500 a month. Together we worked out on paper her net income by deducting the real expenses related to her working, such as taxes, transportation, child-care costs, dry cleaning, and increased giving. We didn't list any of the hidden costs, like the lack of time to clip coupons to save money or the additional costs of dining out. After figuring these costs on paper, we discovered this family was actually spending $1,700 a month so the wife could work at a job bringing in $1,500 a month, resulting in a *loss* of $200 a month. This family did not recognize the real reason there was a shortage each month until we did this exercise together.

Please understand, we're not speaking against wives working outside the home. However, we urge you to figure the true costs.

Consider also whether, if the wife's actual net income is $500 per month and she would like to stay home with the children, there is another way to generate that $500. With technology today, there are many ways to generate income from home. If God has blessed you with children, they are the greatest call on your lives as parents. As a couple, pray for God's wisdom in how you can meet your family's needs while you fulfill your obligations to your children—materially, emotionally, and spiritually—without going into debt.

PLUMB LINE PRINCIPLE

Now if any of you lacks wisdom, he should ask God, who gives to all generously and without criticizing, and it will be given to him.
—*James 1:5 HCSB*

What if I Have Irregular Income?

If you live on commissioned sales or are self-employed, it's likely your income fluctuates. We suggest you take the lowest projected income using your prior annual figures and set up a preliminary budget. Be realistic and conservative in conjuring numbers for your projected revenue and cash-flow amounts—no blue sky! Each month, check and adjust your budget until the numbers work for you. It will be important to build a larger cash reserve than someone on regular income. This reserve will carry you through the low periods. Follow Joseph's example. When Pharaoh put Joseph in charge of Egypt, Joseph wisely stored up grain through the years of abundance, which saved many lives in the land of Egypt and in neighboring nations during the devastating famine that followed (Gen. 41:46–57).

How Do I Make My Budget Work?

You've written down your net spendable income (after tithe and taxes). Next, you've written down your real expenses (be honest!). Next, you've written down your goals. How do you use this information to plan your budget? You've reached step 4 in the recipe and, ultimately, step 5.

Once you have your preliminary numbers, you will see the truth of how much you are overextended. The very first commitment you must make is that you won't borrow anymore, and second, you will pay off your debt. Ask yourself (or your spouse if you're married), "In what areas can we cut back our spending?"

PLUMB LINE PRINCIPLE

How blessed is everyone who fears the Lord, Who walks in His ways. When you shall eat of the fruit of your hands, You will be happy and it will be well with you.
—Psalm 128:1–2 NASB

One area may be dining out. A nationwide survey reports that American families are spending as much as 40 percent of their household money on eating away from home.[3] Some families who want to attain financial freedom faster give up discretionary items like cable television (averaging about $450 per year), multiple magazine or newspaper subscriptions, and other interesting, but not truly necessary, expenditures. Putting needs first, such as housing, clothing, food, transportation, a reserve fund for annual expenses, savings for emergencies, and paying off accumulated debt all take priority over elective expenses. Be honest with yourself and your family and shave off whatever extras you can in order to match your expenses to your net spendable income. If the figures still don't balance, then you need to make those hard decisions. Can you lower your housing costs, drive a less expensive car, take the children out of an expensive school, look for a better paying career, generate additional income? Please remember while making these decisions, you must keep a proper balance in your life, marriage, and family priorities.

At first you will need to track your spending closely until it becomes automatic. We suggest that you manage your budget on a weekly basis until you establish these new habits. If you're married, it's important that you do this together so you both keep on track and remain accountable to your commitment to being good stewards of God's resources.

A budget is really a spending and saving plan. It puts you in charge, rather than letting your desires control you. It also puts you in a proactive position, helping you prepare for those upcoming expenses so you can manage them with confidence and peace, rather than in the helpless reactionary position from which you've been used to operating. Remember, if you aim at nothing, you will hit it every time. A budget gives you a target and creates focus in your finances.

In Conclusion

So what is the recipe to financial freedom? Pray first, then identify your spending habits, list your goals, create a spending and saving plan (budget), and then follow your plan. You will break those old habits and experience God's peace regarding the money He entrusted to you.

You will also begin to fulfill your role as God's steward. "Who then is the faithful and sensible steward, whom his master will put in charge of his servants, to give them their rations at the proper time?" (Luke 12:42 NASB). The outcome is the sweet reward of hearing Christ say, "Well done, good and faithful slave. You were faithful with a few things, I will put you in charge of many things; enter into the joy of your master" (Matt. 25:23 NASB).

Application

PLUMB LINE PRINCIPLE
I have planned it, surely I will do it.
—Isaiah 46:11b NASB

What has God been talking to you about as you read this chapter?

What steps do you need to take to complete a written budget?

What cuts do you need to make in your monthly expenses or lifestyle?

Are you working to your capacity or do you need to research a career change?

If applicable and desired, what steps need to be taken so your wife can quit working outside the home?

What are your deadlines for completing your new goals?

CHAPTER 8

CHILDREN'S BEDROOMS

Children and Money

"Come, you children, listen to me;
I will teach you the fear of the LORD."
—PSALM 34:11

"They who seek the LORD shall not be in want
of any good thing."
—PSALM 34:10 NASB

How soon can parents begin teaching their children about money? As soon as they say, "I want . . ." Children learn by example and experience. They also need instruction in becoming good stewards and wise money managers. In this chapter we will share our journey in teaching our own children, explain how a parent's behavior influences the child's beliefs about money, and describe several important principles you can teach your children along with a list of suggested activities by age group.

How We Learned

One Sunday morning we scurried into church, and I (Debbie) reached into my purse to collect some change for the girls to give in the offering. Like most children, they delighted in dropping coins into the offering plate as it passed by. This Sunday, however, a lightbulb went on in my head. *What kind of message am I sending my children?* I thought. *Is giving loose change out of my purse the principle I want them to learn about giving?* In that moment I realized we needed to teach our children the same financial principles God was teaching us.

As we talked and prayed about teaching our children, we realized there was a lot more to teach them than just the principles of giving. About the same time, Mothers of Preschoolers groups and parenting groups started inviting us to teach their participants about money and children. So, as we taught those groups, we learned. In addition, as we taught parents how to talk with their children about money management, the Lord seemed to use this venue to show those same parents what they really needed to know about managing their own personal finances.

Now it's your turn. We hope this chapter will show you how to share these same principles and practical applications with your children.

Attitude and Actions Are Caught, Not Taught

It starts with you. Your children are forming attitudes about money every day, much of which is based on watching you. Your actions speak volumes to your children. Here are several ideas for teachable moments:

Tithes and offerings: Do your children see you giving your tithe at church? Do they see you giving offerings (above the tithe) to other Christians, missionaries, or worthy organizations that do God's work? Our children know we support the work of other ministries, missionaries, and Christian organizations. They watch us support and care for the poor, those in prison, widows and orphans, pro-life causes, those who help defend the family and religious freedoms, and many other worthwhile causes. As a family, we pray for these organizations each week in addition to supporting them financially.

If you've come to recognize your role as a steward rather than as an owner of the money God has entrusted to you, and you've made a commitment to give 10 percent back to Him, then the next step is to talk with your children about tithing. Perhaps for family devotions you could read the Scriptures together that were discussed in chapter 3 ("Foyer/Entryway: Stewardship versus Ownership") and chapter 6 ("Dining Room: Charitable Giving, Tithes, and Offerings").

Checking account and credit cards: One afternoon our family was shopping, and our daughter Julie asked for a new coat. We explained that we didn't have the money right then to get her the coat. She suggested, "Just write a check." We realized she didn't understand a check must be backed up with cash in our bank account. After returning home, we sat down together and explained the process. Unless parents explain checking accounts or credit to children, they innocently think we receive merchandise or services for free since they usually do not see us reconcile the bank statement or pay the credit card bill. Think of the lifelong benefit you bestow on your children by teaching them these very basic life skills, wrapped in what the Bible says about how to manage money.

Lifestyle: Are you maintaining a standard of living that your children will expect for themselves when they grow up? For example, some families insist on buying or leasing a new car every year. Others shop at the most expensive stores and wear only name brands or designer clothes. What expectations are we inadvertently giving our children? What happens if your daughter marries a man who is called into ministry work and who may not be able to provide her with similar things? Or your son, who may learn to live up to a certain lifestyle rather than listen to God's call on his life?

Attitudes: Ask yourself, "What is my attitude toward work?" Do you find it's easy to put off getting things done? Do you play the lottery, or do you have a wish to get rich quick? Do you stay home for most family meals, or are you always on the fly, catching dinner at the nearest fast-food restaurants? Do you work long hours, rarely seeing your spouse or your children? If you asked your family these questions, how would they answer them?

Whether we realize it or not, our attitudes and actions send daily messages to our children. We transfer our example to them without even being aware of doing so. To train our children in the ways of the Lord, we must begin by asking the Lord to change us first. Boy, isn't that a painful prayer? It all begins with us!

PLUMB LINE PRINCIPLE

For each tree is known by its own fruit. . . . The good man out of the good treasure of his heart brings forth what is good; and the evil man out of the evil treasure brings forth what is evil; for his mouth speaks from that which fills his heart.
—*Luke 6:44a, 45 NASB*

Principles and Knowledge Need to Be Taught

The Bible says, "Train up a child in the way he should go, Even when he is old he will not depart from it" (Prov. 22:6 NASB). Our responsibility as parents is to train and teach our children the principles of God. It is our children's responsibility to choose or reject them. Following are some basic financial principles you can begin implementing with your children.

The Law of Sowing and Reaping

It's no mystery that if we plant corn seeds we will get a crop of corn. If we plant tomato seeds, we will get tomatoes. This is the natural law of sowing and reaping. The same holds true for the spiritual realm. The Bible tells us, "For whatever a man sows he will also reap, because the one who sows to his flesh will reap corruption from the flesh, but the one who sows to the Spirit will reap eternal life from the Spirit" (Gal. 6:7b–8 HCSB).

One of our friends endured a monthlong stay on her back in the hospital before her baby was born. I (Debbie) went to visit her, expecting a bored and frustrated woman. Instead, I found her cheerful and enthusiastic. She showed me what she'd been doing to keep busy. She had written thank-you notes to everyone who sent flowers and letters of encouragement to people in her church. She had been talking to other patients, nurses, and hospital personnel about the Lord and reading devotions and other Christian material to people in the hospital. She was even crocheting a baby blanket to give as a gift.

While visiting with her, I realized she was a living example of sowing and reaping. Instead of focusing inwardly on how boring and depressing her situation might be, she chose to focus outward, looking for ways she could be a source of light to others around her. She sowed joyfulness and reaped joyfulness in her soul and on her countenance.

The same is true with our finances. If we clutch tightly to our money and do not share it with others (because we worry about having enough for tomorrow or don't have what we think we should), we reap worry, discontent, and bondage.

Financial bondage affects not only adults, but in talking with many parents through our counseling and seminar ministry, we've discovered that even children can experience financial bondage. Do you know a child who hoards his or her money, saving it up and not ever spending it, even on something the child might desire? How about the child whose money burns a hole in his or her pocket until the child buys something right away?

You can teach your children the laws of sowing and reaping by planting some grass or bean seeds in a pot. Help them chart the seedlings' progress. Explain that just like the natural law of sowing and reaping, there is a spiritual law of sowing and reaping, and it is just as true in money matters. Read the following Scriptures together and discuss what they mean:

- "The wicked man earns deceptive wages, but he who sows righteousness reaps a sure reward" (Prov. 11:18).
- "He who sows wickedness reaps trouble, and the rod of his fury will be destroyed" (Prov. 22:8).
- "Remember this: Whoever sows sparingly will also reap sparingly, and whoever sows generously will also reap generously" (2 Cor. 9:6).
- "Do not be deceived: God cannot be mocked. A man reaps what he sows. The one who sows to please his sinful nature, from that nature will reap destruction; the

> one who sows to please the Spirit, from the Spirit will
> reap eternal life" (Gal. 6:7–8).

- The parable of the talents in Matthew 25:14–30.

Teach Children Stewardship

We love using this exercise with children. Tell your child that he just received $1,000 and ask what he would do with the money. You may even ask him to write it down. Now tell your child that the money belongs to God. Ask if your child would do anything differently with the money. In most cases the list will change and be totally different! It gives your child a chance to think about money in a new way.

Stewardship is the most important financial principle we can apply to our lives. It is so essential, we believe stewardship should be stressed on a regular basis in every Christian home. For example, when considering a major purchase, pray about it as a family and ask for God's wisdom and direction. In our home we sometimes pray with our children about small, seemingly insignificant purchases. Remember, every penny belongs to the Lord. We and our children will be held accountable for what we spend. Therefore, let's help our children begin thinking like stewards rather than owners.

Teach Children about Tithing and Firstfruits

One of the purposes of tithing is to learn to fear the Lord, to respect His sovereignty (His ownership over us). Even young children are ready to learn about God's principle of providing for His church and the members of the body of Christ. We began teaching our daughters about tithing at a young age, and we followed through with our sons as well.

Our first lesson started when Julie was four years old. She earned $20 modeling for one of the major department stores in Seattle. Our neighbor, the ad layout editor for the company's catalog, had asked if she could use Julie in a photo shoot for the children's section. We thought it would be a fun event and so agreed. When it came time to cash her first paycheck, we asked the bank teller for twenty one-dollar bills. Since this was the first income Julie had ever received, we saw this as a good opportunity to teach her about tithing.

We sat at the table together and counted out ten piles of bills, setting two dollars in each pile. We showed Julie some key Bible verses about tithing and explained how giving to our church helps support the people who work there and pays the monthly expenses. We moved one of the piles to the side and said, "This is how much a tithe is, one-tenth. One tenth of twenty dollars is two dollars." We pointed to the nine piles, then to the single pile off to the side. "You can take this to church next Sunday and put it in the offering plate."

She looked at the nine piles of bills on one side, and back to the one pile that represented her tithe. Pointing to the single pile she said, "Is that all I give to the church?" To Julie, the one pile wasn't enough. Boy, was that a lesson for us.

This exercise not only taught Julie about tithing but also firstfruits giving. God's Word tells us in Proverbs 3:9–10, "Honor the LORD with your wealth, with the firstfruits of all your crops; then your barns will be filled to overflowing, and your vats will brim over with new wine." We showed Julie how to give "off the top." The first little pile of her money belonged to the Lord. Paul instructed the Corinthians, "On the first day of the week, each of you is to set something aside" (1 Cor. 16:2a HCSB).

Set Up a Money Management System

Many parents ask, "Should we give our children an allowance, or not?" There are many viewpoints, and we do not feel one is superior over another. We can share what we have done with our children, and you can adapt it any way that is comfortable for you. The most important key is to teach your children money management principles while watching for attitudes that need to be addressed or adjusted.

There are four purposes for setting up a money management system with your children:

1. It will teach them how to *plan*.
2. It will teach them how to *give*.
3. It will teach them how to *save*.
4. It will teach them how to *spend* (wisely).

Therefore, we believe it's important to give children at an early age a set amount of money on a regular basis (an allowance). You may want to start on a weekly schedule. As children grow older, you can pay allowances twice a month or once a month. Just be consistent with the allowance payday.

How much allowance should your child receive? Since you know your child best, consider his or her needs, expressed wants, and your long-term goals for your child's training about money. Many parents start with an equivalent of fifty cents to $1 per year of the child's age with specifics on how the money is divided for giving, spending, and saving.

Some people disagree with giving children an allowance for doing nothing. Some feel it should be attached to chores. Others feel they should give their children an allowance for being part of the family. However, most parents who give an allowance do so because they want their children to learn how to properly manage money.

We came up with a plan that allows our children to manage the money they receive from us yet ties their personal discretionary spending money to some of the chores they do around the house. They are responsible for keeping their rooms clean and caring for their pets. Chores that free up our time are the ones we tie to their spending money. Some of these include vacuuming, emptying the dishwasher, and sweeping the kitchen.

Some parents tell us they don't have the money to give their children allowances. However, it doesn't have to cost any extra money. You are already spending money on your children. When you put a money management plan into action for your children, you simply transfer some of your financial responsibilities to them. Your children learn to budget, save, buy, and disperse the money instead of you doing it for them.

In the beginning you could make your child responsible for buying one clothing item. For us it was Sunday school shoes. This first began over arguments with the girls about which shoes we could afford to buy. So we added this to their list of items they were to purchase for themselves each year. A little of their allowance (about $2 a month) went into a clothing envelope. We simply transferred some of our budgeted clothing money to their allowance. A year later they would have $24 saved to buy a new pair of shoes. They took their envelopes with us to buy the shoes. One of the girls bought the shoes she wanted and spent every dime (maybe even a little of her own discretionary spending money). Our other daughter found a pair of shoes she liked with a matching purse and had change left over. This provided great hands-on money lessons and curtailed some of the parent-child arguments.

We recommend helping your children set up envelopes (our personal favorite) or glass jars for different categories; show them how to divide their allowances by putting a little money into each envelope or jar every week. For example, there could be a church envelope for their tithe, an envelope for short-term savings, and an envelope for long-term savings. This envelope (long-term savings) is not for a car but rather for college, tech school, starting a business, buying a house, etc. They cannot touch it for any other reason. Decide on a percentage of income, rather than a set amount to deposit into this envelope. Hopefully, they will carry this attitude with them into adulthood to help them save for a home and retirement.

Depending upon the child's age, pick two to ten categories for short-term savings. These would include items for which you are transferring some of your provisional responsibilities to them. These categories could include:

1. Clothing and accessories (begin with one item)
2. Gifts
3. Grooming and personal care
4. School supplies and fees
5. Recreation, sports, and activities

6. Books, music, etc.
7. Lunch money, eating out, and snacks
8. Club dues, uniforms, and other expenses
9. Entertainment and outings
10. Auto expenses (payments, gas, oil, etc)

Decide how much money you would normally spend each year in the categories you select. Divide it by the number of months or weeks that you decide to pay, and that amount goes into the envelope. So in reality their allowance may be large, but you have only transferred your responsibility to their care and management. Understand, this is not "spending money" and will need close supervision, depending on the age and maturity of the child. Remember, the goal is to properly train them in the costs of living and good money management.

Money that goes into these savings envelopes can be deposited monthly or every couple of months into a bank savings account or checking (if they are older) in order to earn interest. You may want to help your child invest some of the money in the long-term savings envelope in a mutual fund to teach him about investing. The tithe can be taken to church each week.

It's important for you to understand the maturity level of your child and match an allowance plan to it. When we first started teaching these principles to our daughters, they were very young. The first time we paid allowances we were unprepared. David needed some change, so he went to Christy to exchange dollar bills for the change he knew she had in her piggy bank. When she saw him removing her precious coins to exchange for the paper money, she got extremely upset. He tried to turn it into a lesson on currency, but she didn't buy it.

Another time Christy received a $25 check from her grandparents for new school clothes. When we went to the bank, the teller gave her a $20 bill and a $5 bill. I (Debbie) saw Christy's countenance fall, so I asked the teller if we could please have all the money in one-dollar bills. As the stack of dollar bills grew higher, Christy's eyes grew bigger. She grabbed the money, looked at me, and exclaimed, "I'm rich!"

Allow Children to Make Financial Mistakes

One of the hardest things for a parent to do is allow our children to make mistakes and suffer consequences. When I (Debbie) taught in the public school system years ago, I observed parents who constantly ran to their children's rescue and bailed them out or defended their children's actions at any cost. They tried to buffer or eliminate the pain their children might experience as a consequence of their misdeeds.

Covering for our children's mistakes is one of the biggest hindrances to their development and maturity. As parents, we've faced many times when we wanted to protect our children or "make it all better." That's a natural reaction. But we know the damage we would do in the long run by not allowing our children to take responsibility for their own actions, behaviors, and choices while under our loving care.

When children are still at home and under our God-given authority, this is the time to allow them to make mistakes and bear the consequences. In finances, this usually happens with purchases. When our girls first began their money management system, they bought chewing gum every week with their spending money. It took every cent, and then they didn't have money for anything else. That lasted about three or four weeks before they realized that by spending their money every week, they could not save up for other things they wanted.

When the girls were old enough and wanted to buy ten-speed bikes, we suggested they consider the new mountain bikes that were just coming out. The tires were wider and stronger, making the bike easier to ride on trails when we went camping. However, they insisted on buying the same kind of ten-speed bikes their friends rode.

A year later Julie admitted she wished she'd bought the mountain bike. We refrained from saying, "We told you so," and gave her a smile of condolence instead. She had learned a hard lesson. At first, we were tempted to buy mountain bikes for our next camping trip or even for her birthday that year, but we held off. In doing so, we realized a second benefit occurred because she learned to accept and make do with her purchase decision.

The hardest time we faced in allowing one of our children to bear consequences was when Christy lost an orthodontic appliance. When the orthodontist gave it to her, he told her not to take it out of her mouth and wrap it in a napkin at a restaurant. We advised the girls that if they lost their appliances, they would have to pay for the replacements since we did not have the money for new ones.

However, while Christy was on a field trip with her orchestra group, she wrapped up the appliance at McDonald's and left the restaurant without it. When she remembered later, she went back and searched the garbage bins but never found it. When we learned the replacement would cost $300, we died inside for her. We wanted to shield her from having to pay for it, but we also knew she had a lesson in responsibility to learn. She set up a payment plan with the orthodontist, and he let her pay on it each month. All of her baby-sitting money went toward the appliance until it was paid off. It seems it took forever (and probably seemed even longer for her), but she learned an invaluable lesson, and she grew in taking responsibility for her own actions.

PLUMB LINE PRINCIPLE

We also rejoice in our afflictions, because we know that affliction produces endurance, endurance produces proven character, and proven character produces hope. This hope does not disappoint, because God's love has been poured out in our hearts through the Holy Spirit who was given to us.
—Romans 5:3–5
HCSB

Misuses of Money

If asked, many people would agree that the most important things in life are not really things at all but our relationships with friends and family. As the saying goes, no one at the end of life wishes he or she had spent more time at the office. However, the pressures of our "why-not-you're-worth-it" culture and the seduction of materialism lure us into the game of pursuit and acquisition. This is especially difficult for parents because they want the best for their children, or guilt haunts them for not being available to their family, or they can't say no to their child's material requests when, after all, they haven't been able to say no to their own desires. These internal struggles lead to the misuse of money. Let's take a look at the top three: substituting money for love or attention, giving money out of guilt, and using money to manipulate.

Substituting Money or Things for Love or Attention

Sometimes parents struggle with guilt when they spend too much time at the office or traveling on the road. Trying to replace time with money or things is not the answer. This breeds contempt and ungratefulness in our children.

Instead, we need to examine our priorities so that we spend adequate time with our children. Then when our adult responsibilities require extra time at the office on a project or on the road, we can ask our children for understanding until we get through the temporary situation. Make a date with your children or plan a special family outing and make sure you deliver on your promise.

If it seems you are constantly away from home, however, examine why. If it's because of a demanding employer, or a second job you're holding down, then you may need to examine your priorities. Our children need us. Please don't fall into the trap of substituting money for love.

Giving Money out of Guilt

This is similar to the principle above, but it involves more than just time. We've watched parents who are separated or divorced dole out cash or prizes because they feel guilty for leaving the marriage. They are trying to pay the children for the lack of time or attention. It may make the guilty parent feel better, but it hurts the children and hinders their maturity. The other spouse may feel resentful as well because he or she doesn't have the same resources to give extras to the children.

Sometimes parents of grown children give exorbitant amounts of money or lavish gifts because they feel guilty over past mistakes or their personal behavior (i.e., alcohol or drug abuse, neglect, lack of involvement, poor money management in the past, etc.). Again, money or material things can't heal emotional issues.

Parents of ill or handicapped children are also susceptible to feelings of guilt or blame for their child's condition. They may try to make it up by buying gifts or giving their children everything they desire. This may only produce spoiled ill or handicapped children.

In all these examples, money and gifts are given to alleviate the parent's feelings of guilt. How much better to give out of love, with the child's long-term needs and maturity in mind. How much better to maintain a balanced approach and use common sense, keeping in mind the impact of our attitudes and actions on our children.

Our heavenly Father gives us a wonderful example when it comes to gifts. He gives us gifts we don't deserve, like the free gift of salvation through a personal relationship with Jesus Christ. Keep in mind, His motivation is love, not guilt.

> **PLUMB LINE PRINCIPLE**
> *If I . . . understand all mysteries and all knowledge, and if I have all faith, so that I can move mountains, but do not have love, I am nothing. And if I donate all my goods to feed the poor, . . . but do not have love, I gain nothing.*
> —1 Corinthians 13:2–3 HCSB

Using Money to Manipulate

Every parent wants obedience from his or her child. However, using money, things, and food is not the way to achieve this goal. The most common real-life example is the distracted mother in the store promising her little angel some candy or other reward if he or she will only behave. Of course, the child continues to whine, sometimes even throwing a tantrum or performing some other power struggle demonstration. Although the child is still misbehaving, he or she gets the promised prize at the checkout stand. What did the child learn? To obey? No, the child learned whining gets you what you want.

Not only is the bribe a poor idea to start with, but the parent unintentionally reinforced unacceptable behavior. A bribe is something given to persuade or induce. A reward is something given in return for service or merit.

Another form of manipulation can happen when a stepparent wants the love or acceptance of a stepchild. In some cases the stepparent tries to "buy" these desired responses from the child through cash or gifts. This is still a no-win solution. Such actions tend to breed contempt and ungratefulness.

Pitfalls of Money

As you may now understand, how we use money is often a visible indicator of something going on spiritually in our lives. Following are some areas that can have problems when associated with money. When these exist, we need to look past the symptoms for the root cause.

Outside Pressures

Even if we are perfect parents and do all the right things, our children are still influenced by outside forces. One of the strongest and most constant influences today is the media (television and movies). Harvard economist Juliet Schor found that for every hour of television people watch each week, they spend more money—as much as $208 annually.[1]

At first we might attribute this to exposure to commercials. After all, ads are designed to make us desire the product (breeding discontent) and thereby convince us to spend our money. However, Schor's survey attributes the extra spending to the television programs themselves. Sitcom characters live a lifestyle that they wouldn't actually be able to afford in real life. As consumers, we are drawn to emulate a more extravagant lifestyle that in reality we can't afford.

Peer groups are also a strong outside pressure to your children. Spending predicated by peer pressure is not a money issue but most likely a self-worth issue. By having limited income, your child will learn whether or not his friends are worth the extra work it would take to maintain the lifestyle and toys used by his peer group.

Friends and neighbors can also be an outside influence. You and your children may feel pressure to keep up with your neighbors or friends. Before our daughters purchased ten-speed bicycles, many of the older children in the neighborhood had been given ten-speeds. Then, when one of our daughter's younger friends received a new ten-speed, we felt tempted to purchase new bikes for our daughters. We didn't want them to be left out of the fun. However, the Holy Spirit gently reminded us whose money we were managing and that the money God entrusted to us at that time wasn't to be spent on ten-speed bikes, regardless of what the neighbors were doing.

Christmas can also be a time of great pressure. When children return to school after winter break, they face the temptation to compare gifts. Even as parents, we may wonder how our children compare to other children in their classes.

We have explained to our children the pitfalls of comparison (which can lead to covetousness). They know we decide a gift purchase category amount at the beginning of the year at our annual planning retreat. Budgeting an amount for your family's Christmas spending and sticking to it will provide a new sense of freedom and joy during a time of year that your family should most enjoy!

Impulse Buying

Spending money comes naturally for most people, including our children. Money management systems help control these spending impulses and help train our child to plan and make wise financial decisions. However, what if children receive a significant gift of money or start earning large amounts of money, beyond their basic needs? Maybe your son or daughter loves to spend money the minute it hits his or her pocket. What can you do?

We've had a "spender" or two in our household. We adapted impulse buying rules for adults and used these rules with our children. Only one item at a time can appear on their impulse buy list. If something better comes along, the current item is crossed off before the new item is added. Also, our children know they must wait a specified amount of time—a cooling-off period—before they can buy something on the impulse list. For adults, the suggested waiting time is a month. For our children, we shortened it to two weeks. By the time they were older, we didn't need the lists anymore because they had become wise money managers.

Our children must also shop and find three different prices for the desired item on their impulse lists. This doesn't mean you need to take your little spender out shopping every time she has a whim. We usually priced the items while running regular errands, and it only took a few extra minutes to go over to the aisle that had the items they were considering. We can also help our children research prices on the Internet (with proper adult supervision). The goal in comparison shopping is not only to get the best price but also to teach our children about sizes, colors, quality, and quantity.

When we first started this impulse buying-list rule, our daughters were about six and seven years old. We went shopping for school clothes, and I (Debbie) was waiting in line to pay for our purchases. Julie held up a cute purse and asked, "Can I have this purse?"

"Certainly," I said. "Put it on your impulse buying list."

Two minutes later she showed me something else. "Can I have this?" she asked.

"Yes," I replied calmly, now with a smile, "but first you must put it on your impulse buying list." The ladies standing in line with us listened intently.

A couple of minutes later, Julie came back again with a toy she found. "I really want this, Mom!"

"OK, just put it on your impulse buying list."

She looked at the toy and then up at me. "I hate that list!" she said and marched back to return the toy on the shelf. The ladies watching tried hard to stifle their chuckles.

With an impulse buying list, all of the pressure was off me and on Julie. If she wanted to buy something (which was not prohibited in our family), she could put it on her list, wait two weeks while finding three prices, and if it was still on her list in two weeks (which in most cases it wasn't) and she had saved the money, she could make the purchase. The list helped eliminate me from being the "heavy" and saying no to my children.

Another benefit was that our children no longer looked to us as the providers of all their wants and desires.

Over the years with this system, our children have learned to delay gratification by waiting to make purchases. The impulse buying list also helped our children learn to shop for the best buy. Christy usually had a few items written down and then crossed off her list. Sometimes she waited longer than the initial waiting period, such as the time she decided she wanted a new watch. She saved up her spending money while she shopped and compared prices. When she found the watch she wanted, she had waited several months and had saved the money to make her purchase.

In one situation, Julie knew she was receiving a pet fish as a gift. While we traveled to a convention, the girls stayed with friends of ours, and while shopping with them, Julie researched prices for the extra aquarium accessories she wanted. When we returned from our trip, she showed us the legwork she had put in while tagging along with our friends. Impulse buying lists work for both adults and children!

Stealing and Making Restitution

If your child is very young and took something from a store, be sure to ask if the child understands what he or she did. With all the free samples given out at stores these days, your child may not understand that what they did was improper. Go over these verses in the Bible about stealing, along with the consequences and biblical guidelines of making restitution (quoted from NASB):

- "'You shall not steal'" (Exod. 20:15, Deut. 5:19).
- "And Jesus said, '. . . You shall not steal'" (Matt. 19:18).
- "The thief comes only to steal and kill and destroy; I came that they may have life, and have it abundantly" (John 10:10).
- "You who preach that one shall not steal, do you steal?" (Rom. 2:21b).

- "You shall not steal, nor deal falsely, nor lie to one another" (Lev. 19:11).
- "Will you steal . . . and walk after other gods that you have not known, then come and stand before Me in this house, which is called by My name, and say, 'We are delivered!'—that you may do all these abominations?" (Jer. 7:9–10).
- "There are six things which the LORD hates, Yes, seven which are an abomination to Him: Haughty eyes, a lying tongue, And hands that shed innocent blood, A heart that devises wicked plans, Feet that run rapidly to evil, A false witness who utters lies, And one who spreads strife among brothers" (Prov. 6:16–19).
- "The perverse in heart are an abomination to the LORD, But the blameless in their walk are His delight" (Prov. 11:20).
- "He who steals must steal no longer; but rather he must labor, performing with his own hands what is good, so that he will have something to share with one who has need" (Eph. 4:28).
- "If a man steals an ox or a sheep and slaughters it or sells it, he shall pay five oxen for the ox and four sheep for the sheep" (Exod. 22:1).

Take your child back to the store or to the person to return the item, have them ask for forgiveness from the proper authority and be ready to make restitution. Once your child repays three or seven times back what he or she took, they are far less likely to take something that doesn't belong to them again.

When your child breaks something that belongs to someone else, your child should make restitution. We were not aware of this principle when our girls were young but have since implemented it with our young sons. If one of our children borrows or plays with a toy from a friend and it breaks, they must pay to have it repaired or replaced, using their personal money. Again, keep things in balance. Just as God forgives and restores us, the owner of the broken item may forgive your child and not require them to make restitution. As the parent, you must ultimately decide what the best course of action is should your child face such a circumstance.

Hoarding

What if you have a child who refuses to spend any money at all? This may not sound serious, but hoarding can be as much a problem as spending everything.

First, try to determine why your child is hoarding. It may be the result of greed, a security problem or a sense of selfishness. Read and discuss the story in the Bible of the rich man who built bigger barns and hoarded grain (Luke 12:16–21). His perspective was short-term and self-centered. He failed to recognize that we are given resources here on earth to provide for basic needs and to help others.

After addressing the core spiritual issue, consider using the government approach. Agencies such as the Education Department receive annual budget amounts, which must be spent in the current year. Any left over is cut out of the following year's budget. Adapt this method for your child, perhaps on a per month basis. We saw this technique work with one child, through the process of merely reducing the amount he received the next month. If your child tries to beat the system, you may need to require an accounting of how she spent the money.

Remember to keep balance in trying these suggestions with your children. We focus on the key attitudes in our children and then implement whatever additional training or accountability may be needed to bring things to a proper, biblical balance.

Borrowing Money

We covered the pitfalls of borrowing money and debt in chapter 4, "Laundry Room." But how do you communicate this information to your children? This is more important today than ever, not only to prepare your children for adult responsibilities but also to protect them from aggressive banks and credit card companies in college and now even high school.[2] In a recent survey by Merrill Lynch, 68 percent of the teens who responded said they have never discussed responsible credit card use with their parents.[3]

Our children need to fully understand the dynamics and potential damage of credit and borrowing before they reach adulthood. Spend the time to give them the proper training. You don't have to wait, as even young children can understand the concepts.

I (Debbie) taught an economics class to about twenty five-year-old children in our home school co-op. Most of these kids couldn't yet read. Each week I told a story with a financial principle, or we did an exercise together. The one they remembered most was when I shared about the true cost of a bicycle bought with borrowed money.

I gave the students a choice. They could buy a used bike for $20, which they had the cash to buy. Or they could buy a brand new bike for $120, using the $20 as a down payment and borrowing the $100. For those who chose to borrow, they paid 18 percent interest on the borrowed $100. Since most of them only made about $2 a month, they discovered it would take them almost nine years and another $100 to pay off the bike. They saw firsthand how the bike would cost almost twice the original price.

At the end of the exercise we took a vote. Not one of those five-year-old students wanted to buy the new bike! I ended the session, telling them to remember this story when they were old enough to buy an automobile. I challenged them to always calculate the full and final cost of borrowed money.

When Julie wanted to upgrade her flute, we allowed her to borrow money from her savings account. She agreed not to spend any of her baby-sitting money until she paid back what she'd borrowed into her account. Each time she earned money, she tithed it, put a percentage toward her mandatory long-term savings, and all the rest went to repay her loan to herself. Julie told us during this experience that she now understood firsthand the bondage of debt!

Grandparents

Some parents have shared with us concerns over their parents giving the grandchildren cash and other gifts that the parents would not, or could not, give their children. In other words, the grandparents were giving to the grandchildren without the permission or blessing of the children's parents. Many times this seemingly innocent gesture by a relative becomes a source of frustration.

Grandparents and other relatives need to understand that their well-intended gifts can undermine the authority of the parents. These gifts can also conflict with what the parents are attempting to teach their children through certain circumstances. The problem is compounded when grandparents feel it is their right to spoil their grandchildren. The key issue is really about God's authority structure in the family, not the money or gifts. We feel it can be worked out to everyone's benefit, if certain conditions are discussed (as follows) and met.

One solution might be to set your children up on the money management system described in this chapter. Once in place, it, instead of the parents, becomes the standard. Then share it with the grandparents (or relative) and ask them to participate with you in the system. We suggest you try this cooperative approach before confronting them with the behavior that's causing a problem.

You can also offer helpful alternatives to the large gifts. For example, suggest they set up savings accounts for your children instead of giving them gifts. This savings could be used toward college, making a down payment on a house, or for starting a business when they are older. You could also suggest that the grandparents take the amount of money they are giving or spending and place it in a tax-deferred college fund instead. If the money or gift giving is really a problem, ask the grandparents to spend time, rather than money, with your children. Long-term, that gift of time is probably of more value to the grandchildren than the money. A healthy relationship with a grandparent is a blessing children can never purchase.

If the grandparents decline because they really enjoy giving gifts, perhaps discuss setting a limit on the amount of the gifts. This solution allows the grandparents to continue getting pleasure by giving, and the smaller gifts will not thwart the parents' goals to teach their children about God's provision and lifelong money management techniques.

If you allow your children to accept financial gifts from family members, consider having the children put the money into a savings account initially. This way you can implement the impulse buying list principles discussed earlier, and the money can be saved toward a larger, more meaningful gift or a long-term goal. At some point the child can share with the grandparents or family members how they eventually used the gifts given to them.

There is no easy solution to this matter. It will come down to what is most important to you, your children's well-being, your relationship with the grandparents or relative, and the principles involved. It may even be necessary to risk the short-term relationship in order to ensure the long-term maturity and spiritual development of your children. Use clear and honest communication with the family members involved, expressed in a spirit of humbleness, genuine love, care, and concern.

Suggested Activities

In teaching children how to be good stewards and wise money managers, explain there are three things we do with money: share, save, and spend. There are two kinds of savings: long-term and short-term. For children, long-term savings could be money for college (for adults, it's retirement). For children, short-term savings could be saving for a big purchase (perhaps a new bike, a video game, or later, a car).

Ages Three to Five

Children in this age group are able to make limited choices (between two or three items); they are beginning to understand that money can get things they want, and they generally think a nickel is worth more than a dime because it's bigger and that coins are more valuable than bills. This age group is also ready for attitude and character training. Here are a few ideas you can use with your children to help them at this stage:

- What is money? Show your child how to do coin rub-bings on white paper with crayons or colored pencils, or try colored chalk on dark construction paper. Help your child write the name of each coin and discuss how we trade these coins for things we buy (food, clothes, toys) or for services we use (like seeing the doctor or getting the car repaired).

- What is the difference between coins, and how do they translate to bills (relative value)? Using play money or real money, spread some coins and a few bills on the table, such as one-dollar bills, five-dollar bills, a ten-dollar bill, and maybe a twenty-dollar bill. Let your child sort and stack the pennies, nickels, dimes, quarters, and bills in individual piles. Make it fun! Introduce the idea that ten pennies are worth the same as a dime, four quarters equal a one-dollar bill, and five one-dollar bills equal one five-dollar bill.

- What is it worth? Next time you're grocery shopping, give your child a choice between two kinds of cereals or two kinds of juice. Show him how to look for the price of each. Which one costs more? Which one costs less?

- How much does it cost? Let your children weigh fruit at the store. Explain how you will pay for the fruit based on how much it weighs. See if they can identify the price per pound on the sign or label.

- How can we spend less? Before shopping, ask your children to sort coupons you plan to use at the store. Explain how they will help you spend less for the family. Let them hold the coupons as you walk through the aisles, and let them give the coupons to the cashier.

- How does money work? Play store with your child, using play money and empty food boxes.

Additionally, teach your children we do certain activities to take care of ourselves and our things, such as making our beds every morning and brushing our teeth after every meal and before going to bed. As they get older, look for ways to encourage your children to care for themselves and their belongings. Have them do routine tasks without pay, such as setting the table or putting toys away. Your goal is to help them learn responsibility, respect, orderliness, and stewardship.

Ages Six to Eleven

Many children are ready to receive an allowance by the time they start school, so consider which expenses your child is expected to pay and determine the amount you feel comfortable giving him or her. Some families pay an allowance of 50 cents for each year of age; others pay $1 per year of age. Remember, you are already spending money on your child—why not turn it over to her to manage, so she can learn by experience under your loving guidance?

- If you haven't already, help your child develop a plan for his money—his first budget. Provide four envelopes or four glass jars and let your child make labels for them: "Giving," "Long-term Saving," "Short-term Saving," and "Spending." Later you can add more categories, but this is a good way to start. Explain how these will be used and how much money you expect your child to put in the envelopes or jars by adapting these suggested percentages: 10 percent, tithe; 40 percent, short-term savings; 25 percent, long-term savings; 25 percent, discretionary spending.

- Continue looking for ways to help your children develop their sense of responsibility and belonging in the family. Make a short list of chores. Promote camaraderie and cooperation by setting a timer while they do their tasks at the same time every day.

- Encourage entrepreneurial endeavors. Help your child set up a lemonade stand and offer additional goodies for sale. Make your next garage sale a family affair and allow your child to keep money she earns from the sale of her personal items; tell her you plan to donate your items left afterward to a local charity and encourage her to do the same. Provide change so your child can divide her earnings into her four jars or envelopes.

- Teach your child the difference between ownership and stewardship. If your child's school has a class fish or pet, arrange with the teacher for your child to take care of the animal over a weekend. Also, when visiting the bank, explain to your child how the bank manager takes care of the money your family deposits there and how this is similar to God giving us resources to manage for Him.

- Encourage a spirit of giving by modeling it for your children. As a family, sign up to sponsor a child in another country and talk about the child you're helping. Describe the other country and living conditions and how the money is used to help this child. Display the child's picture on the wall. Ask your children to draw pictures to send with your letters through the agency.

- Provide opportunities for your child to earn extra money by doing a task you don't have time or energy to do.

- Pay promptly, and assist your child in dividing the money between the four jars or envelopes.

- Call local banks and credit unions to find the best deal for your child to open a savings account. Make weekly trips so your child can deposit his long-term savings. Show him how to keep track of deposits and interest earned in his own bank book or on the computer.

- Teach children how to compare prices while shopping for something they want.

- Look for opportunities to help your child learn how to recognize needs versus wants.

- Focus on delayed gratification and the benefits of saving.

Ages Thirteen to Seventeen

At this stage your child yearns for independence and wants to make earning and spending decisions without your assistance. However, he or she still needs help in discerning the difference between needs and wants. Your teen is also now able to deal with abstract concepts. He or she can set goals and make plans to reach those goals. Your teen may try to borrow money (from you or friends) to satisfy wants, which should be discouraged, based on Scripture.

- Involve your child in family financial discussions about what to buy, how to save more, how to cut expenses, and groups to which the family will contribute.
- Review your child's allowance and make any adjustment if necessary.
- Show your young teen how to compute miles per gallon on the family car.
- If your teen is employed, help her prepare her income tax return.
- Continue encouraging generosity while emphasizing stewardship versus ownership. Let your child see you sharing your time and resources with others. Encourage him to participate in volunteer activities and to continue tithing.
- Help your teen create a more detailed budget with savings categories for clothing, activities, and entertainment. Car expenses (fuel, insurance, oil changes, etc.) also should be discussed and included in your teen's budget.
- Teach your child about investments. Play the "stock market game" by choosing a company to follow in the newspaper or online; pretend to purchase $100 worth of stock and chart its activity for a month. Make it a competition by choosing a different company to track. Who lost or gained the most money? After this practice month, help your child purchase real investments if he shows interest.
- Discuss the use and abuse of credit cards, the real cost of credit, and the danger and despair of financial bondage. Learn about the history of credit, and your teen may be surprised at the difference in how our society views credit today.

- To demonstrate to your child the real costs of living, use Monopoly money to show how much you must pay for taxes, housing or rent, insurance, auto expenses, utilities, food, clothing, and savings. Be sure to take 10 percent off the top for giving. We guarantee your son or daughter will be shocked at what it takes to pay for a family's needs and how little is actually available for discretionary spending!

- Choose a "Plumb Line Principle"—a Scripture related to money—to study as a family each week (many are listed throughout this book).

In Summary

What are the important principles we should teach our children about money?

They need to learn to budget. When they become adults, they will choose whether they will continue using a budget, but it's our job as parents to teach them how to do it. In our family, our younger children do not live in a democracy; they live in a benevolent dictatorship. Until they reach the age when we believe they're accountable, budgeting is not optional.

They need to learn to tithe. While our children are young, we require our children to tithe. When we feel they reach the age of accountability, we release them, and this issue is between them and God. We first teach them the biblical principle of tithe and offerings and help them develop the pattern of giving. Ultimately, it is a heart issue, not a money issue.

They need to learn to save. We have always required our children to set aside 25 percent of everything they earned for long-term savings. At first they didn't like it, but we knew it would reap big dividends for them. For adults, long-term savings can be for buying a house or for starting a business. For our children, this may launch them into something they want to do in the future.

They need to learn to discern between needs and wants. First, we parents must be careful about giving our children everything they want. It's not healthy and can lead to an attitude of entitlement and selfishness. God doesn't give us everything we want. As our children gain experience by managing their own money, they will begin to understand the distinction between needs and wants.

They need our time, attention, and example. This is perhaps the most important. We parents must not substitute money for our love or time. This is so easy to do when both husband and wife work. Examine your motives and don't use money to replace your time or to manipulate or bribe your children.

The bottom line for children? Spending time with *you*—laughing, loving, and learning. So make time to teach them about God's financial principles even as you begin modeling these principles in front of your children.

Application

PLUMB LINE PRINCIPLE

These commandments that I give you today are to be upon your hearts. Impress them on your children. Talk about them when you sit at home and when you walk along the road, when you lie down and when you get up.
—Deuteronomy 6:6–7

What has God been talking to you about as you read this chapter?

Are there changes you need to make?

How will you begin teaching your children about money management? Set a date and write it here.

What tools or forms do you need in order to begin?

Where have you failed your children and need to ask forgiveness?

CHAPTER 9

DEN

Savings, Investing, Wills, Retirement, and More

You are God's field, God's building . . . as a
skilled master builder I have laid a
foundation. . . . But each one must be careful how
he builds on it.
—1 CORINTHIANS 3:9-10 HCSB

Welcome to the den. This is the part of the house where we discuss important matters such as savings, investing, insurance, retirement, wills, and inheritance. Please understand, we are financial teachers and counselors, not investment or insurance professionals. However, our advice comes from the experts we've talked to, the materials we've read, the experiences of friends, and the decisions we've made. When it comes to specifics, you will need to research and develop your own unique theories. However, it's important to know some basic principles related to these areas of our financial lives and to measure our actions against what God's Word (the Bible) has to say.

Savings

Is saving scriptural? Absolutely. God's Word says, "There is precious treasure and oil in the dwelling of the wise, But a foolish man swallows it up" (Prov. 21:20 NASB). Saving is part of God's economy. He even built it right into nature, since the ant knows to store up provisions for the winter (Prov. 6:6–11).

When we toured the entryway in chapter 3, "Stewardship versus Ownership," we discussed Christ's parable of the stewards and their talents of money (Matt. 25:14–30). In verse 27, Jesus said the master told the servant he should have at least put the master's money in the bank and earned interest on it. That appears to be God's minimum stewardship requirement.

We introduced you to the idea of savings when we were in the kitchen and discussed budgeting. There are four basic categories or levels of savings:

- The reserve fund (saving to spend, short-term savings)
- The savings fund (sometimes called emergency savings or a rainy-day fund)
- Investments (long-term savings)
- Retirement savings and pension plans (for the future)

First, there is the reserve fund. This is money you set aside for paying annual or semiannual insurance premiums, for medical co-payments and deductibles in the coming year, for auto maintenance and repair, and for household appliance repair or replacement. This first level of savings is used to pay these irregular expenses throughout the year. The lack of saving for such real expenses is many times the catalyst that pitches people into consumer or credit card debt. They simply didn't count all the expenses in a full year. They only added up the sum of their monthly bills, food costs, auto fuel, and other regular expenses. But you can do it right by adding up *all* your expenses and setting aside a portion each month as reserve savings.

The next level of savings is for those less predictable expenses. The semiannual car insurance premium bill is a given; the bill arrives every six months. The car breaking down is another given, although a little less precise in due dates. Additional challenges include an employment layoff or a large medical expense that insurance doesn't completely cover. How much should we save for this category of expenses?

Sometimes people ask it this way: "Should we have two weeks' salary in savings, one month's salary, or three months' salary?"

Our answer is a simple yes. If you haven't started a savings plan for these types of expenses, then start by setting aside a regular amount until you've saved one week's salary. When you've saved one week's salary, start working toward two weeks' worth. When you have two weeks' salary saved, work up to one month's salary and so on, until you hit the level of savings you feel you need for your personal circumstances and job situation.

Your vocation will also dictate the level of savings you need. For instance, one of the largest employers in the Pacific Northwest is the Boeing Company. Unfortunately, layoff notices have become fairly common there as elsewhere, which means employees should be prepared in the event of a layoff or loss of employment, by setting aside savings to cover living expenses between jobs. The Northwest also lives up to its reputation for an abundance of rain, which is tough on those who work in an outdoor trade. Generally, these employees can count on working steadily for nine or ten months of the year and then need two or three months' worth of savings.

This savings principle is true at all levels of income. Our friend and Dave's longtime Covenant Group member Norm Evans, executive director of Pro Athletes Outreach, has stated that it takes the average pro athlete about two years to transition out of athletics back into the real world. As a result, a pro athlete needs about two years' savings in the bank.

There can be unpredictable financial challenges for most people working in a ministry. The economy experiences ups and downs, and then events such as the tragic September 11 terrorist attacks cause further economic fallout. Our ministry, Barnabas, is no exception. We've also faced challenges with regard to revenues and income. Had we not been practicing these principles in this book, including saving money for low periods of ministry donor revenues, we would have never made it through the difficult times.

Interestingly, people don't have a problem saving *too* much for unpredictable expenses. No one has ever called us and asked, "What do we do with our excess savings?" The real problem comes from the reverse situation, when people call and say, "Dave and Debbie, we've been out of work for thirty days. We don't have any savings. What should we do?"

Saving for the future protects us from unpredictable events or emergencies. However, the personal savings rate in our nation is approaching zero for the first time since the Great Depression.[1] Ten years ago American families saved about 9 percent of disposable income. Today that figure has plunged to nearly zero[2] while consumer debt continues to rise to historic levels. This is not healthy and cannot be sustained for long. Remember, debt causes the borrower to become a servant to the lender (Prov. 22:7).

Have you ever heard the phrase "double-tithe"? Many of our parents and grandparents knew this concept. The idea is to give 10 percent of your income to God (first), then save the next 10 percent for yourself. Obviously, if most people followed this simple principle, they would be in a much better financial condition. However, many people are under the impression that if they can't save a lot of money from each paycheck, there's no use in trying to save even a small amount. This is unfortunate.

This may be you. You may wonder, "How can I save money when I can barely make ends meet?"

Don't be discouraged. Just start by saving $10 per month. Human nature being what it is, many people are not able to meet the challenge to save $20 per month until they discipline themselves to save that first $10 per month. So, as the Nike ads say, "Just do it." For most, it's simply a matter of priorities; take a long-term perspective on your future lifestyle versus immediate gratification of today's desires.

Also, if an unexpected bill causes you to skip one of your savings payments, don't give up. Just get back on track with the next paycheck. And if you face an emergency and have to dip into your savings, don't be discouraged. That is why people have savings—to provide funds for emergencies.

Take time to examine your situation. Is something keeping you from saving money? What is it? Are you counting the cost as the Bible instructs you to do? Are you making the hard, important decisions? What action do you need to take to get to the point where you have some savings?

PLUMB LINE PRINCIPLE

In the house of the wise are stores of choice food and oil, but a foolish man devours all he has.
—*Proverbs 21:20*

Investing (Long-term Savings)

Some ask, "Is investing scriptural?" We believe the Bible indicates it is. In Matthew 25:14–30, the banker is again used as an illustration. Bankers invest the money you and I give to them. They invest it in businesses, stock markets, and other investments. Ecclesiastes 11:1–2 tells us, "Cast your bread on the surface of the waters, for you will find it after many days. Divide your portion to seven, or even to eight, for you do not know what misfortune may occur on the earth" (NASB). In other words, invest some money and don't put all your investments in one basket.

What should we invest in? For that, you will need to do some additional research. However, let us share a few basic principles.

First, you need to know your reasons and goals for investing. It's helpful to write them down. Most people's goals usually center on providing for themselves financially throughout their lifetime, primarily for those retirement years. They may also have goals to fund educational costs, traveling, helping children, funding God's work, and providing an inheritance. These are many of the major reasons given for investing. Some of these will be addressed later in this chapter.

Regarding investments, remember to monitor your motives and attitudes. The Bible offers the following warnings:

- Ecclesiastes 5:10—"Whoever loves money never has money enough; whoever loves wealth is never satisfied with his income."

- Proverbs 18:11–12a—"The wealth of the rich is their fortified city; they imagine it an unscalable wall. Before his downfall a man's heart is proud."
- Proverbs 23:4–5—"Do not wear yourself out to get rich; have the wisdom to show restraint. Cast but a glance at riches, and they are gone, for they will surely sprout wings and fly off to the sky like an eagle."
- 1 Timothy 6:9, 17–19 NASB—"But those who want to get rich fall into temptation and a snare and many foolish and harmful desires which plunge men into ruin and destruction. . . . Instruct those who are rich in this present world not to be conceited or to fix their hope on the uncertainty of riches, but on God, who richly supplies us with all things to enjoy. Instruct them to do good, to be rich in good works, to be generous and ready to share, storing up for themselves the treasure of a good foundation for the future, so that they may take hold of that which is life indeed."

Notice that in the last passage above (1 Tim. 6:9, 17–19), Paul does not condemn wealth in any way, although he warns against desiring to "get rich." He also gives instructions to those who have already gained wealth. As Christians, we are in a battle for people's eternal lives, and battles take money—lots of it. God's Word does not call Christians of our day to a life of poverty. Remember, the key is our heart attitude about money. Desiring wealth for money's sake will bring temptation and a snare (1 Tim. 6:9). The Bible also says money can sprout wings and fly away (Prov. 23:5).

PLUMB LINE PRINCIPLE
Let not a rich man boast of his riches; but let him who boasts boast of this, that he understands and knows Me.
—Jeremiah 9:23b–24a NASB

A basic investment principle that has become less remembered today as a result of greed and get-rich-quick attitudes is a simple but powerful principle: Even a little amount of money saved over a long period of time reaps big dividends. Children today could become millionaires if they save a little bit of money over a long period. The problem is we don't start saving the little amount of money!

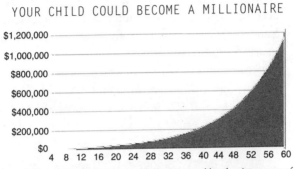

YOUR CHILD COULD BECOME A MILLIONAIRE

This chart shows the growth, compounded at 8% monthly, of an investment of $100 per month beginning at age 4 and ending at age 18, assuming that the investment remains untouched until age 62. This investment is hypothetical and does not represent the performance of any actual investment.

Copyright © 2002 Standard & Poor's, a division of The McGraw-Hill Companies, Inc.[3]

Furthermore, if you were to start saving $2,000 each year and your money earned 4 percent annually (far below the market's average of 10 percent over a long period of time), then the chart below shows what you would accumulate after ten years, twenty years, and thirty years (above inflation):

THE ADVANTAGE OF STARTING EARLY

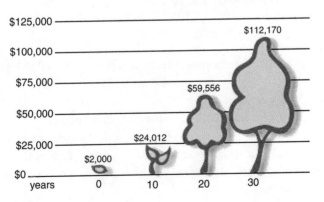

Published by the American Savings Education Council (ASEC).[4]

Small amounts put aside regularly can yield big returns as a result of compound interest. For example:

- A person who saves $10 a week for five years in an account earning 5 percent interest, then increases that to $20 a week for the next five years, can accumulate nearly $10,000 in a decade.

- A person who increases the savings rate to $40 a week for the next 35 years will end up with more than $250,000—$80,600 invested and more than $170,000 earned in interest.[5]

YEARS TO REACH ONE MILLION DOLLARS

MonthlySavings	2%	4%	6%	8%	10%	12%
$50	177	105	77	61	51	44
$100	144	88	66	53	44	39
$150	125	79	59	48	40	35
$200	112	72	54	44	38	33
$250	102	67	51	42	35	31
$300	94	62	48	39	34	30
$400	82	56	43	36	31	27
$500	73	51	40	33	29	25
$750	58	42	34	29	25	22
$1,000	49	37	30	25	22	20
$1,250	42	32	27	23	20	18
$1,500	37	29	24	21	19	17
$2,000	30	25	21	18	16	15
$2,500	26	21	18	16	15	13
$3,000	22	19	16	15	13	12
$4,000	17	15	14	12	11	10
$5,000	14	13	12	11	10	9

Chris Snelling, http://www.free-financial-advice.net/make-million-dollars.html (8/26/02)
Used with permission

Another basic investment principle is this: You need to know and understand your risk temperament. We are different individuals and have different tolerances for risk. Ask yourself, "If I make this investment, will I be able to sleep at night?"

Are you controlling the investment, or is the investment controlling you, your thoughts, and your emotions? One of the best investment advisers out there is *you* because only you know your risk tolerance.

Once Dave's mother woke in the middle of the night bothered by an investment. The next day she sold the investment because it was starting to control her thoughts and emotions. She ended up selling that investment at nearly the highest price the investment had ever obtained. To this day it is one of her fun investing stories, and she would tell you she was led by the Lord in that decision to sell.

PLUMB LINE PRINCIPLE
The LORD will accomplish what concerns me; Your lovingkindness, O LORD, is everlasting.
—Psalm 138:8a, NASB

When it comes to learning about investing, there are many good books, Web sites, and experts to learn from. When someone asks us for an investment adviser referral, we tell them, "We can send you to ten different investment advisers, all of whom we believe are living their lives according to God's financial principles, but we guarantee that all ten of them will offer you a different financial plan, and all ten can lose your money in the blink of an eye!" That's because it's called "investing," and risk is part of the dynamics involved.

Before you start investing, do some homework. Learn the language. You can do it. Understanding some of the basics is not as complicated as you might think. You can learn about terms like "large cap stock," "index fund," and others by visiting Quicken's helpful Web site at http://www.quicken.com/glossary/. It lists dozens of terms in alphabetical order with detailed definitions.

Look for other opportunities to learn. Probably any day of the week in a metropolitan area, you can go to a free seminar on investing. The presenters will give you a lot of education on the subject. However, there is one word you need in your vocabulary when you go—the word *no*. Chances are there is a pretty good salesman up front giving the presentation. Take the free education but get yourself out of the room without signing anything. Even if you like the product being sold, it's smart to give yourself a cooling-off period.

Sometimes at these investment seminars you'll hear that investing is like building a house or a pyramid. The word picture is a good one and epitomizes the concept of this book. When building a house, you start from the ground floor and work your way up. You can't start in the attic. With investing, the ground floor is your budget. You also need a savings account. You need to get life insurance in place, disability insurance, and any other insurance coverage you feel is important. These are all ground-floor items.

PLUMB LINE PRINCIPLE
Do not wear yourself out to get rich; have the wisdom to show restraint.
—Proverbs 23:4

We have several friends in the investment field, and people come to them and say, "We just received a $150,000 inheritance; what should we do with it (i.e., what investments should we buy)?" After these advisers review the person's finances, they sometimes counsel, "There are some things you should take care of first before buying stock or making major investment decisions. We recommend that you buy some short-term CDs (certificates of deposit) or invest in a couple of money market funds while you get your ground floor established—set up a budget, start an emergency savings plan, and obtain any recommended insurance coverage. After you take care of these needs, come back to see us. Then you'll be ready to make investments."

Get the ground floor established first. Once the ground floor is in order and your immediate needs are funded, then you are ready to move up to the next floor—and start investing long-term. On this floor, start with CDs and money market funds. Not much return, not much risk. Today people tend to skip this floor. They jump floors to the higher-risk investments. Many of these people who jumped floors had a rude awakening when the economy slumped in 1999 and the early 2000s. So protect yourself and your future.

When that second floor has an appropriate amount of money set aside on it, now you move up to the next floor, mutual funds. Mutual funds provide more of a chance for higher return on investment but also more risk. Until recently many people did not really understand how much risk is involved in mutual funds, and many did not think they could go down in value!

When that floor is set to the level of investment you decided is appropriate, you're ready to go to the next floor. At this point we are usually talking about buying individual stocks. There is a much higher chance of return, but again, there is also a much higher risk.

Once that floor is set and appropriately invested, you're ready to go up into the attic. Usually we are talking precious metals, venture capital, commodities, initial purchase offers (IPOs), etc. These are appropriately called high-risk investments. There is a small amount of room in the portfolio for these investments (for some people but not for everyone—remember your risk temperament). However, you have to build your floors wisely and in order. It is usually a mistake, long-term, to skip floors.

Again, you need to do some research and seek out the professionals who can help you become educated and better informed with regard to investing. There is always something new to learn, but do yourself and your family a favor by getting familiar with the basics before you start investing, just to protect yourself. In this instance knowledge truly is power.

Hoarding:
When Saving Goes Too Far

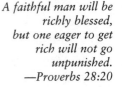

PLUMB LINE PRINCIPLE
A faithful man will be richly blessed, but one eager to get rich will not go unpunished.
—*Proverbs 28:20*

When it comes to long-term savings, be mindful of hoarding. It's truly unfortunate we live in a society that's sometimes driven by greed, and hoarding can become a problem. There are people today who have saved up so much money it seems as if they believe they will live to be 650 years old. That's called hoarding. There must come a time when we ask ourselves, "How much is enough?"

When is the house big enough? When is the car new enough? When is the vacation long enough? When do I quit consuming that with which God has blessed me?

If you don't ask yourself these questions, it will never be enough. Take time to decide right now, "This amount ($_____. Choose a number and fill in the blank.) will be the limit of my lifestyle spending. After this level of income, anything God blesses me with will go right back into His work.

PLUMB LINE PRINCIPLE

And He told them, "Watch out and be on guard against all greed, because one's life is not in the abundance of his possessions."
—Luke 12:15 HCSB

I will simply give it away." You see, if we don't set a limit, it will never be enough.

Insurance

Health Insurance: To avoid or neglect to carry health insurance today is to live on the brink of financial disaster. The unknown *can* happen. It only takes about one hour in a hospital to devastate a family financially. God's Word tells us we are to provide for our families (1 Tim. 5:8), and in our current economy, that should include health insurance.

In discussing health insurance, we want to be sensitive yet truthful. Health insurance has, without a doubt, grown to be very expensive. For many people, their employer funds a major portion of their insurance premiums. For those who don't have this benefit, health insurance is a large monthly expense to fund. Yet health care coverage must be resolved, or we leave our families and ourselves vulnerable to the consequences of enormous medical bills.

Usually people who do not have health insurance come to that conclusion by default. They let circumstances dictate their choice not to carry health insurance. They are short of money, or they are unemployed for a time, or they didn't make enough business profit, or any number of other reasons. Instead of dealing with the bottom-line truth issues—such as, cutting less-important expenses, living more frugally, raising their income, looking harder for employment or a new career, changing the way they do business, etc.—they don't make these hard decisions and slowly default until they reason to themselves that they are a victim of circumstance and so eventually stop funding their health insurance. Remember, our finances are talking to us every day. Are we listening to the facts and acting on the truth?

Also, any person could potentially go through a season when they need help from others (including covering health insurance premiums). That's when we as Christians can step in to help others out for a month or two (Phil. 2:4). However, that help should be for a short season, and we need to keep accountability as part of the process (Gal. 6:5). Sometimes, there are longer seasons of need because of extended illness, injury, or other extenuating circumstances. The body of Christ should be there if the need is legitimate and not a result of personal neglect.

PLUMB LINE PRINCIPLE
Each of you should look not only to your own interests, but also to the interests of others.
—Philippians 2:4

That's why every church should have a financial ministry that includes education, accountability, benevolence funds, food pantries, clothing exchanges, and career tools.

As health insurance costs rise, insurance premiums become harder to fund. However, this simply means we need to be quicker to respond to financial circumstances, be more in tune with our family's needs and our businesses, and be more aware about possible alternatives.

For Christians, other caring organizations may work for you as alternatives to health insurance. Check out any alternative plan thoroughly. Understand how it works and how it does not work. You need to know if it's the right program for you and your family. Usually alternative programs require you to carry catastrophic health care coverage at a high level of deductibility. Find out the laws governing your state. You need to take responsibility for the research, your decisions, and the results.

Life Insurance: We believe life insurance is a viable means of provision today for Christians and their families. A real-life example is the New York man who added a $275,000 term life insurance policy to his investment mix, due to his concern about keeping his kids in college if he died before they graduated. The carrier paid his claim after he was killed at his desk at the World Trade Center on September 11, 2001.[6] If a husband were to die tomorrow, how would he provide for his family? That's what life insurance is for.

The Bible says we are to provide for our families. We don't have the same inheritance system today that we see in the Bible.

We don't have the same passing on of businesses from one generation to the next, and when we do, there can be high tax consequences. Families don't live in the same house generation after generation. And in our culture it's not typical for families to pitch in financially to help each other out. However, we are still instructed to provide for our families, so for us, life insurance is another way to meet that responsibility.

How much life insurance should we have, and what type do we need? As with investing, you need to seek the counsel of professionals you trust. Spend sufficient time educating yourself and understanding the basics.

PLUMB LINE PRINCIPLE

He who tills his land will have plenty of food, but he who follows empty pursuits will have poverty in plenty.
—Proverbs 28:19 NASB

You first have to learn the language being used in the field before you purchase insurance. Do you need whole life, term life, or universal life? How much insurance coverage do you need? Do you need to insure your spouse? What about covering the children? What bells and whistles fit your needs or wants and your budget? Once you understand the basic insurance language you can compare plans.

We encourage you to contact three insurance agents or brokers you think you might want to do business with. Talk with them about your needs and see what direction they advise you. What kind of insurance do they recommend, at what amounts of coverage, what extra features (the bells and whistles), and at what cost? From these three agents or brokers you should start hearing some common themes or common recommendations.

Once you have a good idea of the kind of insurance you need, the amounts of coverage, and the terms that best fit your needs (and any extras you may want), then go back to each agent or broker and say, "Quote me on this (stating your specific requirements), and please don't vary from my specified requirements at all." After receiving their quotes, you will be able to compare apples to apples and oranges to oranges and make the best buy.

With any insurance purchase, make sure you're dealing with a reputable, financially healthy company. You want a company that will still be around ten, twenty, or thirty years from now. Insurance reporting firms such as www.AMBest.com, can help you obtain this kind of information.

When it comes to deciding how much life insurance you need, we suggest this basic formula. Take the income that you may need to replace and multiply it by ten. For example, let's say the husband is making $40,000 a year, and let's assume Social Security will pay $10,000 a year in survivor benefits. This means he needs to replace $30,000 per year in income ($40,000 less the $10,000 provided through Social Security). Take the $30,000 and multiply it by ten ($30,000 x 10 = $300,000). He will need $300,000 in life insurance coverage.

The idea is to provide the surviving spouse the $300,000 to invest at a 10 percent return and thereby generate $30,000 a year of revenue (never touching the principle of $300,000). If a 10 percent return is too high of a rate or risk, then you have to use a larger multiplier (like eleven, twelve, or whatever figure provides the annual income you need).

When you make appointments and talk to insurance professionals, they will help you think through other factors. What about money needed to bury the spouse? How about money you might need to pay off the house mortgage or to educate the children? These are all good questions you should think through and decide.

When it comes to the high cost associated with burying a loved one, we recommend the People's Memorial Society. It cost us $15 for a one-time, lifetime membership (with no additional membership fee for children under the age of eighteen). It guarantees us a simple burial or cremation (without a graveside service) for less than $900. This fee can rise (and does), but it's still very low compared to thousands and tens of thousands of dollars spent on caskets and funerals. Understand, the cremation or burial fee does not cover the burial plot. It simply covers picking up and preparing the body, placing it in a simple casket (or cremating the body if so desired), and delivering it to a local cemetery. You can obtain more information on your computer by going to www.peoples-memorial.org Web site.

Disability Insurance: For many people, disability insurance may be needed more than life insurance. Disability insurance pays you monthly income if you get injured or become disabled. It tends to be much more expensive than life insurance, so it's easy to overlook the benefits and never make the purchase. Again, your professional insurance agent or broker can help you establish your needs and shop for what's best for your situation.

PLUMB LINE PRINCIPLE
Do not be overawed when a man grows rich, when the splendor of his house increases; for he will take nothing with him when he dies.
—Psalm 49:16–17a

Retirement

Many are surprised to learn that today's concept of retirement does not appear in the Bible. The idea of retiring to relax, travel, or play golf every day is not reflected in God's economy. In fact, we've only found one mention of retirement in the Bible. It is found in Numbers 8:25–26a, and it only addresses the Levites, God's ordained spiritual leaders of that day: "But at the age of fifty years they shall retire from service in the work and not work any more. They may, however, assist their brothers in the tent of meeting, to keep an obligation, but they themselves shall do no work." There is no other mention of retirement in the whole Bible.

PLUMB LINE PRINCIPLE
Make plans by seeking advice.
—Proverbs 20:18a

We believe God has work for us to do until the day He takes us home. Now clearly we can't expect to do the same things at the same physical intensity at age sixty that we were able to do at twenty-five, so it's wise to plan for this type of change. That change may involve volunteer work or full-time or part-time ministry. Every church, Christian ministry, charity, or volunteer organization needs people who can help. Who carries more life experience and may have garnered the wisdom and discernment earned over a productive lifetime? Our seniors and retirees. Many of them can offer so much more from their experience than the younger generation can. We need them active and involved in all aspects of our lives—physically, emotionally, and spiritually.

This does not mean when we reach retirement that we can't travel and see the wonderful world God has made. This does not mean we can't play a few rounds of golf. This doesn't mean we can't take a few extra naps. The key is our focus. Is our focus on ourselves, or is it on God and serving Him in whatever area He might choose to use us and the talents and skills He's given us, which will bear eternal fruit in others' lives?

PLUMB LINE PRINCIPLE
And this is my prayer: that your love may abound more and more in knowledge and depth of insight, so that you may be able to discern what is best and may be pure and blameless until the day of Christ, filled with the fruit of righteousness that comes through Jesus Christ—to the glory and praise of God.
—Philippians 1:9–11

Wills and Trusts

Eventually, everyone needs a will or trust. Unfortunately, about half of all Americans die without one.[7] If you don't prepare a will, the state steps in and dictates its will for your assets and children. And in most states it's not a very good will.

This is one of those necessary expenses of life. Most people need only a simple will, a boilerplate type. You don't have to decide who gets the pictures on the wall, who gets which dishes, who will get Grandma's quilt, or other such details. You can make those decisions later. Such details are not usually a part of the basic components of your will. They are addendums to your will, and you can easily change them as the need arises.

A will may cost a couple hundred dollars, depending on where you live, who you go to, and what you want done. Some people need to establish a trust of some type. This is usually based upon your assets, taxes, liabilities, and other factors. Your local professionals can help you determine your specific needs.

Seek the counsel of an attorney or estate planner who specializes in wills and trusts. We've seen some estate planners go into a church and do wills in a group setting for very low fees as a service to the church members. They figured out a process to help many people at once and yet offer personalized service to address specific needs.

We also recommend that you write a letter to your spouse that starts, "When I die, here's what I think you should do." Then finish the letter, expressing your specific instructions. As part of this same process, each spouse should know all the financial details of the household and estate, including budgeting. Each spouse should know how to balance the checking accounts and where all the important papers and documents are located.

PLUMB LINE PRINCIPLE

An indecisive man is unstable in all his ways.
—James 1:8 HCSB

Place this information in a special binder, whether the information or document is an original or copy of an item that may be in a safe deposit box. It is also wise to have some of the mature children know these facts and details, just in case both parents die together or within a close period of time.

There are many products available in the marketplace to help you get organized in this important area. We have all heard sad and unfortunate stories of spouses being caught off guard when the other spouse dies. Don't let this happen to you. Take whatever action is necessary to get a will or trust completed, get all the necessary documents in order, and have a written plan for the surviving spouse and children.

Inheritance

Here is a difficult topic that may involve strong emotions. Some have asked, "If it is all God's money, do I pass it on to my children who don't know Him?"

You are the one who has to answer that question for your family. Actually, we can argue it from Scripture both ways, but in the end you will have to answer it for yourself. Hopefully, you have raised your children in God's Word, and they are committed Christians, so this question is easily resolved. However, if you know your children are going to go out and blow the money, should you pass it on to them? Incidentally, the average inheritance today lasts only eighteen months. It seems rather sad that the parents save their whole lifetimes, and their adult children can burn through the money in one and a half years.

In one real instance, we know someone God prospered abundantly who went to his children and said, "This is God's money, not mine. How much of it you get will be based upon what I see from your life." He chose tough-love words. He also told them that he would spend the time necessary to make sure they were educated and trained to be good stewards. That's good parenting!

In another instance we once heard someone say he would base the inheritance upon the amount of Scripture each of his children had memorized. This approach packs a load of wisdom behind it.

PLUMB LINE PRINCIPLE
A good man leaves an inheritance to his children's children.
—Proverbs 13:22a NASB

If we examine the Bible for examples, parents didn't typically give the money to their children *after* they died; many times it was distributed *before* they died. Fortunately, the children held their parents in such high esteem and honor that they dutifully took care of their parents until their parents' deaths. We (Dave and Debbie) both like this biblical Old Testament approach because the firstborn received a double portion of the inheritance. Guess what? We're both firstborns! However, siblings probably wouldn't think this approach was such a hot idea. Also, that double portion carried additional responsibilities calling for a high level of maturity.

In our culture today most people pass on any inheritance upon their deaths. As parents, let's fulfill our responsibility and make sure we have trained our children to be such good stewards of God's funds that it makes it down to the grandchildren and great-grandchildren. When this happens, the inheritance is now perpetual and is a continual blessing to all.

Application

What has God been talking to you about as you read this chapter?

PLUMB LINE PRINCIPLE
Though your riches increase, do not set your heart on them.
—*Psalm 62:10b*

What action do you need to initiate and what changes do you need to make?

What professionals do you need to seek to assist you?

What are your timelines for your new plans?

CHAPTER 10

LIVING ROOM

Making Your
Plan Work

The mind of man plans his way,
But the LORD directs his steps.
—PROVERBS 16:9 NASB

C ome to the living room and have a seat. What have we
learned so far? In the entryway (chap. 3), we learned
God is the Owner of the earth and everything in it,
including us (Deut. 10:14; Ps. 24:1; 1 Cor. 6:19–20). He expects
us to manage His resources He put into our care (Luke
16:10–11). However, we Americans have not recognized our
roles as stewards; instead, we've been living as owners and now
suffer from affluenza and its consequences—one of which is debt
(Gal. 6:7–8).

In the master bedroom (chap. 5), we learned how husbands
and wives view money differently. We saw God's design for couples to work as a team (Eph. 5:21). We also discussed giving and
tithing in the dining room (chap. 6), which is not only outward
evidence of our role as stewards but also reveals an inward attitude of gratitude toward God (Prov. 3:9).

In the kitchen (chap. 7), we learned about God's recipe for
financial freedom and budgeting (Luke 14:28). And in the chil-

dren's bedroom (chap. 8), we learned how to teach our children God's principles of finance.

So how do we implement everything we've learned and make it part of our lives? That's the purpose of this chapter in the living room—setting goals and making your plan work.

First, Pray

God is not only the owner, but He's also the Master Architect. Are you functioning as an owner rather than as a steward? Do your dreams need to be modified in light of God's ownership and His master plan? Money is the testing ground of our choices, our character, and even our theology. How you handle money is a tangible indicator of your relationship with God, and your bank statement serves as an exact index of your life.

PLUMB LINE PRINCIPLE
For the eyes of the Lord are toward the righteous, and His ears attend to their prayer.
—1 Peter 3:12a
NASB

Spend some time alone with God. What do you need to lay on the altar? In other words, what do you need to give back to God? Yourself? Your family? Your current possessions? Your employment? How about your future? Take time to pray and do this now.

Second, Write Down Your Goals

It's easy to let life just happen. Deep down inside, however, many people harbor dreams and aspirations. Some are realistic, some are not. What are yours? Let's discuss this at a practical level. Specifically, what would you like to achieve in the next twelve months? A year from now, what would you like to be able to say you accomplished in the past year? How about five years from now?

Take a few minutes now to write down your ideas, then list the steps you might need to take to accomplish them. List your goals for one year from now, and then five years from now. If you don't write them down, you won't have a target, and without a target, you won't have anything to aim for. Most likely, you desire to make some changes. That's probably why you're reading this book.

Consider including your spiritual goals too. When we started out in financial ministry, we were aware that most churches used the New International Version (NIV) of the Bible, so we decided to use it, with a twist: I (Dave) read all the way through it and underlined and highlighted every passage in that Bible dealing with money. Just about the time I finished, Larry Burkett called. As a field representative for his ministry, I listened to Larry explain that he wanted all the field reps to use the same version of the Bible (until then, we could use the version of our choice). He chose the New American Standard Bible (NASB). Debbie and I both owned an NASB, a version we used for more than seven years serving as leaders in Bible Study Fellowship. However, my NASB wasn't marked and highlighted for finances like my NIV, so I laughed and thought, *Well, I guess God wants me to read through the Bible again.* And so I did.

PLUMB LINE PRINCIPLE

My son, give me your heart and let your eyes keep to my ways.
—Proverbs 23:26

What are your goals spiritually? Financially? Vocationally? To meet your financial goals, will you need to get additional training or change vocations? If so, how will you go about it? Write everything down.

Another area for goal setting is your relationships—toward your spouse and your children. Do you spend individual time with each person in your family? Maybe this could be one of your weekly goals. How about hospitality goals? Perhaps you could invite different families over for dinner once a month and bless them by sharing your house and food with them. Bottom line, we are asking you to think of your goals in light of being a steward of everything God has entrusted to you.

As you prepare this list of goals, you may discover that your long-range goals will influence your short-range goals. For instance, your goals for five years from now will have steps that start now and build on what you accomplish in the next twelve months. And the goals you have for the next year depend on what you do next month. Your choices today affect tomorrow and, thus, your future.

For financial goals, jot down your ideas now, then complete the following sections. You'll have a clearer picture of your financial situation.

PLUMB LINE PRINCIPLE
Then the Lord answered me and said, "Record the vision And inscribe it on tablets, That the one who reads it may run. For the vision is yet for the appointed time; It hastens toward the goal and it will not fail."
—Habakkuk 2:2–3a NASB

What you're doing is developing a plan. By the time you finish working through this chapter, you will have a list of five-year goals, one-year goals, and the steps you feel you need to take to accomplish them. You will have a plan, and you will know how to make your plan work.

Next, Take Inventory of Your Debt

Make four columns on a sheet of paper. In the first column list your creditors. In the second column list the total amounts you currently owe to each. In the third column list the monthly payments owed. In the fourth column write the interest rate for each. Now you have two choices for your pay-off plan:

1. You can choose to pay off your smallest balance first, and then take that payment and add it to the next debt to speed up payoff, and so on.
2. Or you can choose to pay off your highest interest rate balance first and apply that payment to the next debt to speed up payoff, and so on.

The advantages of paying off the smaller balance first is the rush of accomplishment you will experience, and it frees up money sooner to add to the next debt payment.

Go on a credit fast. If you stop using credit and pay off your existing debt using either of the above methods, you will experience the peace that comes with financial freedom.

Prepare a Monthly Spending Plan—Your Budget

Make a list of your monthly expenses, including housing costs, utilities, food, and household, personal, and debt payments. Don't forget to include a monthly amount for those annual bills like insurance, auto registration tabs, property taxes, etc., which you will set aside in your reserve fund. You can keep these reserves in your savings account until those bills come due. In addition, figure an extra amount for those predictable but untimely expenses, such as auto maintenance and repair, medical and dental expenses, and so on. Even $10 per paycheck will give you a start in protecting you from future debt. Later, when you've paid off your consumer debt, you'll be able to build this savings account for new goals, like a vacation. Then, at the top of this monthly spending plan, put 10 percent for tithe.

PLUMB LINE PRINCIPLE
"Is this not the fast which I choose, To loosen the bonds of wickedness, To undo the bands of the yoke, And to let the oppressed go free And break every yoke?"
—Isaiah 58:6 NASB

Add up the total. If your expenses exceed your net spendable income (the amount you have each month after tithe and taxes), you will have to make adjustments. For several ideas, see chapter 4: "Laundry Room: Debt." Bottom line, your expenses cannot exceed your income—after all, that's what got you into debt in the first place. Remember, this belt tightening is necessary until you free yourself from debt. And don't forget—the amount you pay on accelerated debt payments will be free of obligation after you pay off those creditors!

PLUMB LINE PRINCIPLE
Direct my footsteps according to your word; let no sin rule over me.
—Psalm 119:133

As we mentioned earlier, your long-range goals dictate your short-range goals. Just for illustration, let's say you want to retire with a million dollars. A financial planner will spend two or three hours of your time and help you figure out how much money to save, starting next month. If you save that amount of money each month, you will reach your goal. You see, that's how your long-range goals dictate your short-range spending and saving. If you don't start, you'll probably never reach your goal. If you do start, you'll most likely reach your goal.

George Santayana (1863–1952) wrote, "Those who cannot remember the past are condemned to repeat it." Don't repeat your past. Instead, learn from it, and improve your future by working on your goals. By going through this chapter, you should have a list of short-term and long-term goals, your financial debt repayment plan, and your monthly budget plan written out in detail. Now you know what you need to do, starting with the next paycheck. This is where you need to start. Eventually, by working the plan, you'll be able to raise your eyes and see how far you've come. Don't forget what God's Word says: "The mind of man plans his way, but the Lord directs his steps" (Prov. 16:9 NASB).

Let God find you faithful of planning your way, while allowing Him to direct your steps.

Application

PLUMB LINE PRINCIPLE:
I run in the path of your commands, for you have set my heart free.
—Psalm 119:32

What has God been talking to you about as you read this chapter?

What changes do you need to make?

Whom do you need to seek help or counsel from to overcome hurdles or obstacles?

When will you start your new plan?

CHAPTER 11

GUEST ROOM

Single-Parent Families

For I am the LORD, your God,
who takes hold of your right hand
and says to you, Do not fear;
I will help you.
—ISAIAH 41:13

Take a break and join us in the guest room as we discuss the serious needs of single-parent families. In America today there are 105 million households (282 million people).[1] Of those, 12 million are single-parent families.[2]

In our ministry we have counseled many single parents. Divorce or the death of a loved one is devastating for them and their children to deal with, both emotionally and financially. But no matter how they came to be a single-parent family, we as Christians need to be especially alert and sensitive to these members of our population because it's tough enough on them already.

In addition to emotional support, money is the number-one concern for single parents. When many families spend 35 percent or more of their income on housing, a single parent may face spending as much as 85 percent of their average income for housing and child care needs. Creating a livable budget seems impossible, and many single parents slide deep into credit card debt trying to make ends meet. However, a budget is vitally important, particularly when money is scarce. Remember, a budget is simply a plan for how money will be managed, saved, and spent. Setting up a budget helps you identify areas of spending you can cut back on in order to avoid debt. You may decide you need more income to meet your family's needs (food, shelter, and clothing), so a change in employment or training may be a consideration. A budget helps you decide how to meet your family's immediate needs and gives you a sense of discipline, direction, and control. It also keeps you focused at a time when simple survival may feel overwhelming.

The financial principles we've discussed in this book can be used by anyone regardless of their status. God's principles work for everyone—single adults, married couples, teenage entrepreneurs, and single-parent families. Go back and review the chapters on budgeting (the kitchen), debt (the laundry room), stewardship versus ownership (the foyer), giving (the dining room), and how to make your plan work (the living room).

In this chapter we'll share specific tips addressed to single parents, and then we'll share ideas others can use to help the single-parent families they know.

If You're a Single Parent

You have faced many challenges, the most likely ongoing one being money. It probably seems there is always more month at the end of the money, and at the end of every day you feel exhausted. You not only now serve as breadwinner, but your children depend on you for transportation, food, clean clothes, medical care, entertainment, and a clean home. No wonder you feel exhausted! Here are several ideas to help you cope:

- Recognize that you can't do it all, all the time. No one can. If the dirty dishes must sit in the kitchen sink until tomorrow so you can read a story to your children at bedtime, followed by a hot bath for you while your favorite music plays softly in the background, so be it. Your kids—and you!—are worth it.

- On your next day off, sit down with your checkbook, bills, and a pad of paper. It's time to get brutally serious about your budget. In one column list your expenses. In the second column list your debt. Pray for God's guidance in how to manage the resources available to you. Examine your spending. Does it exceed your income? What can you live without, even temporarily until you get back on your feet? Look closely and honestly. Many families find they can free up hundreds of dollars a year by making conscious, committed changes in their spending choices.

- Make a plan to pay off any credit cards or loans. The freedom and peace you'll feel are intoxicating, putting you in control.

- It's tempting to charge purchases when money is tight, but don't do it. Commit to a debt-free lifestyle and trust God to provide for your family's needs.

- Start saving for emergencies, even if it's a small amount each paycheck. Remember, cars and appliances wear out, illness strikes, visits to the doctor require deductibles or co-payments. Be prepared. Remind yourself, "It's not a matter of if, but when."

- Find ways to save time and energy as well as money. Cook from scratch, double the ingredients, and freeze the extra for those busy nights when you're tempted to pick up dinner at a fast-food restaurant. Make a list and run your errands together. Involve your children with Saturday morning chores—set a timer and make it a game. Gather up outgrown clothes, unused toys, and extra household items and donate them to charity (get a tax receipt if you itemize on your tax return).

- Make your children feel extraspecial by planning regular fun time with them. Play a board game, visit the library together, or play at a park. Plan a theme night for dinner, like Mexican, and dress up in hats and blankets while eating tacos. None of these ideas cost money yet will produce priceless memories for you and your children and energize your relationship with them.

- Take care of yourself too. Trade child care time with another parent so you can pursue a hobby, enroll in a class, or take a rejuvenating walk.
- Give your self-esteem a boost by connecting with new friends. Join a church, participate in a Bible study, attend (or start) a parents' support group.
- To save money, barter your skills for services you need. Some single parents offer cleaning, sewing, or computer skills in exchange for legal services, baby-sitting, painting, lawn care, or automotive repairs.

PLUMB LINE PRINCIPLES

"For I know the plans I have for you," declares the LORD, "plans to prosper you and not to harm you, plans to give you hope and a future. Then you will call upon me and come and pray to me, and I will listen to you. You will seek me and find me when you seek me with all your heart."
—*Jeremiah 29:11–13*

As a father has compassion on his children, so the LORD has compassion on those who fear him.
—*Psalm 103:13*

As a single parent, you face emotional and financial challenges. God's Word offers comfort and direction. In Psalm 34:15 we read, "The eyes of the LORD are on the righteous and his ears are attentive to their cry." This theme carries through to the New Testament: "Humble yourselves therefore under the mighty hand of God, so that He may exalt you in due time, casting all your care upon Him, because He cares about you" (1 Pet. 5:6–7 HCSB).

Also, don't be afraid or embarrassed to ask others for help. Your situation gives the body of Christ the opportunity to respond in love, care, and financial backing. At the same time keep your expectations realistic. Today God's people are not giving as the Bible directs, so that makes for a shortage of funds for many real and urgent needs.

Most of all, take God at His word. Come to Him with your concerns, and surrender your future to Him. He welcomes you with open arms.

Ministering to the Single Parent

Single parents live in our neighborhoods; their children attend school with our children, and many worship beside us in churches across the country. We can serve as conduits of God's love by ministering to these families in tangible ways. Here are just a few ideas:

- Offer to watch the children for a couple of hours, giving the single parent the gift of time (and the feeling of support!).
- Help single parents find high-quality, low-cost child care for when they're at work. If your church doesn't have a child care center, consider proposing and organizing one. Maybe the Lord will use you to meet this need through your church.
- When you hear the parent is ill, drop off a hot meal or a pizza.
- Before a shopping trip, call and ask if you can pick up anything.
- Call the utility company and make arrangements to pay one month's cooling or heating costs for the family. We know people who do this on a monthly basis, like supporting a missionary or ministry.
- Mail a card of encouragement.
- Drop off a bag of groceries and laundry supplies anonymously.
- Involve your church—organize a team of workers who can volunteer services once a month, such as auto repair, lawn care, and painting or home maintenance repair. Remember, single parents have no one to help with the honey-do list of chores. A church we know developed a ministry dedicated to keeping single parents' cars running and safe on the road.
- If you know a Christian dentist or doctor, talk to him or her about this family. Arrange care at a reduced or free rate. Give the family's phone number or address to the

care provider so the office can contact the family
directly.

- Invite another family to join your family for a popcorn-
and-movie night at your home.

- Help start a financial ministry at your church that
trains, encourages, and equips people (including single
parents) in proper stewardship and budgeting.

- Offer to mentor a single parent on their finances, to
hold them accountable. Please take special note: It's not
appropriate for a male to hold a single-parent female
responsible, or vice versa. Same gender accountability
mentors are encouraged in the Bible.

**PLUMB
LINE
PRINCIPLE**
*I tell you the truth,
whatever you did
for one of the least
of these . . . you
did for me.*
—*Matthew 25:40*

- Please don't treat single parents as poor
money managers. Few people can live on the
average single-parent's income and make
ends meet.

- Most of all, express understanding.
Single-parent families are sorting through a
lot in the first year or two. Be sensitive,
patient, and encouraging.

Application

What has God been talking to you about as you read this
chapter?

If you're a single parent, what changes do you need to
make?

What things are in your control that you can work on?

What things are out of your control and need surrendering
to God?

What specific goals do you need to make and what resources
do you need to pursue?

Who can help hold you accountable for making hard decisions?

If you're not a single parent, in what ways can you help one near you?

PLUMB LINE PRINCIPLE
May he give you the desire of your heart and make all your plans succeed.
—*Psalm 20:4*

CHAPTER 12

GARAGE

Repairs and Maintenance

He whose walk is blameless
and who does what is righteous,
who speaks truth from his heart . . .
who does his neighbor no wrong . . .
who keeps his oath even when it hurts,
who lends his money without usury
and does not accept a bribe . . .
He who does these things will never be shaken.
—PSALM 15:2-5

I n the garage we store tools, keep repair materials, and accumulate items for future use. We keep bicycles, sports and camping equipment, and yard care items. It's also where we generally carry out many of our household and motor repairs. Once upon a time a garage was used to park the family car. Today it seems you have to have a three-car garage in order to have enough room to park one car. Does this mean people fall victim to accumulating more and more stuff? It seems we never have enough garage.

In this chapter we want to review the rooms of our financial house, discuss important repair and maintenance tips, and give you final words of encouragement.

Get Your Toolbox
and Revisit the Rooms

Have you ever seen a house in the middle of construction? Contractors don't build and completely finish one room at a time. After the foundation is laid, they build the framework and complete the house in stages according to a blueprint. Later, in remodeling or making improvements, the homeowners get their toolbox for the tools needed to work on specific projects. They may also find themselves in those same rooms again and again, changing window treatments, repainting, repairing trim, patching walls, or working on new projects during their time in that home.

These activities are true for personal finances. Houses aren't built in a day, and neither is your financial house. It also saves time and money to follow a plan for maintenance and upkeep. If you've never made a plan for your future before, this book is your first tool to help you accomplish that goal. Go back and answer the questions at the end of each chapter. Use the worksheets included in the appendix. Develop a budget, which is really your spending plan to help you gain control of how you share, save, and spend the money that God entrusts to you. Make a master list of things to do and review it on a daily or weekly basis. Keep the list updated and follow your due dates. If you need outside help or counsel, find the person who can help you. And most importantly, review the "Plumb Line Principles" from your most important tool for life—God's Word, the Bible.

PLUMB LINE PRINCIPLE

Unless the LORD builds the house, They labor in vain who build it; Unless the LORD guards the city, the watchman keeps awake in vain.
—*Psalm 127:1 NASB*

How often should you review your progress? How often should a husband and wife meet to discuss budgets and spending?

There is no right or wrong answer to these questions. We suggest you review your budget and spending patterns often. Spouses should meet as often as necessary so that each spouse feels comfortable with the communication and the process. This may start out to be once a week and later evolve to once a month or quarter.

In our family, we also schedule an annual "review and planning retreat." We arrange care for our children so we can have a weekend to ourselves to pray and plan our finances for the coming year. We strongly advocate this for all married couples. Where you go for your retreat and how much or how little you spend depend on your own financial circumstances. Many years we had very little money for our retreat. This gave us an opportunity to be creative, and it was just as enjoyable.

In the start-up phase (preparing for your budget retreat), talk about your concerns. Be willing to communicate about your financial plan daily or weekly and whenever the process gets bogged down. Work as a team, with the victory of financial freedom as your goal. Above all, do not let guilt, blame, or fear stop your progress. Encourage each other with the truth that you're working together to be good stewards of God's resources. Remember, He loves you. "'For I know the plans I have for you,' declares the Lord, 'plans to prosper you and not to harm you, plans to give you hope and a future.'" (Jer. 29:11–12). He wants the best for you. Be encouraged—and be an encouraging helper and friend to each other!

When you start tracking expenses and living on a budget, we urge you to schedule time to talk at least once per month. It may even be important to meet weekly until these new disciplines become a habit. Look at your spending amounts and compare them to your budget. Talk about the categories in which you overspent or any problem areas. If the pressure is on, remember to use kindness and gentleness in the process. Decide on the steps you should take to resolve the problems or conquer any hurdles in your way. Make sure you write them down. Include to-be-completed dates as needed. Also ask yourselves, "Do we need outside counsel with this, and who can give us such help?"

Once your budget is up and running, how often you and your spouse meet will depend on circumstances, levels of trust, and accountability needs. Initially, we recommend that the main bookkeeper give the spouse a monthly report or printout of income and expenses, highlighting any areas of concern. You may find that after a season you can go to quarterly reporting. It may be that you progress to the point where you only need to come together for a meeting when you start to overspend or need to make some adjustments because of new expenses that surface and need to be addressed.

The key goes back to what we suggested earlier: Meet however often is needed so that both of you feel comfortable with the communication and the process.

If you're single, find an accountability partner (discussed at length under "Safety Instructions" in chapter 2, "Tools of the Trade") and agree to meet on a regular basis.

What to Watch For

Be on the sharp lookout for discouragement. As you work on getting your financial house in order, you are making a bold, conscientious step toward God and service to

Him. The enemy is going to do everything possible to bring discouragement your way. Satan doesn't want you to be free to serve God. He wants all of us living in mediocrity and financial bondage. He's working overtime against us so we'll get discouraged, give up, and fall back to our old ways.

PLUMB LINE PRINCIPLE
Now the Lord is the Spirit; and where the Spirit of the Lord is, there is freedom.
—*2 Corinthians 3:17 HCSB*

The true cost of living, even in something as basic but necessary as going to the grocery store, can be terribly disheartening. This process you have begun will take some time as you learn new habits and apply God's principles. This is actually a change that should last for your lifetime. It may require letting go of something you have been holding onto with all your might. However, becoming free from things that bind us requires sacrifice. Let go, and walk each step toward freedom!

- "You, my brothers, were called to be free. But do not use your freedom to indulge the sinful nature; rather, serve one another in love" (Gal. 5:13).

- "I run in the path of your commands, for you have set my heart free" (Ps. 119:32).
- "Now the Lord is the Spirit; and where the Spirit of the Lord is, there is freedom" (2 Cor. 3:17 HCSB).

Watch out for discouragement. We have seen this over and over in counseling others. Just about the time you decide to get your finances in order and start budgeting, the first month into the process your car breaks down or the refrigerator stops working. Don't let the enemy use unexpected difficulties to make you throw in the towel and say, "Oh, this doesn't work. I quit!" Look discouragement square in the face and persevere. Don't give up! Call a friend (or even a professional if you feel it's that serious) who will help pick you up, dust you off, start you on the road again, and cheer you on in the process.

PLUMB LINE PRINCIPLE
Before I was afflicted I went astray, but now I obey your word.
—Psalm 119:67

Be Careful of Overreacting or Overcorrecting

Sometimes this can be more of a male tendency. "All right, we're going on a budget. We're going to get this budget balanced today! No more food, no more clothes, no more entertainment, and no more spending until we are out of debt."

If we overreact, our spouse will probably cringe and dig in his or her heels knowing we are out of balance. If we overcorrect, the frustration of total curtailment will burst and cause more overspending than had we just tried to reduce.

Give Yourself and God Time

Remember, how old you are is how many years you've had to accumulate habits. Give yourself time to make changes. Give God time to renew your mind and build in new disciplines as you study His Word, apply His principles, and work on your finances.

You don't get into difficult financial circumstances in one day, in one week, or sometimes even in one year. So don't expect to resolve everything in a short amount of time. Relax, take a deep breath, and press forward one day at a time. Faithfully fulfill your financial responsibilities and then trust God for the bigger picture. He loves you and wants to do a mighty work in your life.

PLUMB LINE PRINCIPLE

Do not conform any longer to the pattern of this world, but be transformed by the renewing of your mind. Then you will be able to test and approve what God's will is— his good, pleasing, and perfect will.
—Romans 12:2

Step Back and View the Big Picture

Sometimes we are so caught up in our everyday circumstances that we lose sight of the bigger picture. We can't see how far we've come. As you keep records, take a step back and review your progress. Use those little victories to cheer yourself on and continue. Keep remembering God is bigger than your current circumstances, and He can give you back all the years the locusts have eaten (Joel 2:25), and much more (Job 42:10).

PLUMB LINE PRINCIPLE

How blessed is everyone who fears the Lord, Who walks in His ways. When you shall eat of the fruit of your hands, You will be happy and it will be well with you.
—Psalm 128:1–2 NASB

Seek Counsel When You Need Assistance

Many people can sense when they need extra help. Seek out those individuals within your church or community who can give you godly counsel or practical assistance. Don't let pride keep you from seeking the help of others.

- "Where there is no guidance the people fall, But in abundance of counselors there is victory" (Prov. 11:14 NASB).
- "Plans fail for lack of counsel, but with many advisers they succeed" (Prov. 15:22).

- "Therefore let him who thinks he stands take heed that he does not fall" (1 Cor. 10:12 NASB).
- "Pride goes before destruction, a haughty spirit before a fall" (Prov. 16:18).
- "God resists the proud, but gives grace to the humble" (James 4:6b HCSB).
- "The prudent see danger and take refuge, but the simple keep going and suffer for it" (Prov. 27:12).

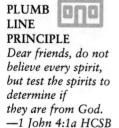

PLUMB LINE PRINCIPLE

Dear friends, do not believe every spirit, but test the spirits to determine if they are from God.
—1 John 4:1a HCSB

When you seek counsel, use discernment and weigh the advice in light of God's Word. Remember, it's our responsibility to seek God's Word for His answers. We, not a third-party counselor, are ultimately responsible for our actions and the consequences.

If your church doesn't have an active financial ministry, maybe God is calling you to become involved. Over the years we have worked with Larry Burkett and Crown Financial Ministries to train laypeople to teach and counsel, as well as help churches expand their financial ministries. You could get the ball rolling at your church!

Think Creatively to Pay Off Debt

There are times when it may be necessary to sell some assets in order to reduce debt or carry you through a time of low income or reduced revenues. We encourage people first to make sure they have considered the bigger-picture issues along with any root causes before selling assets. Otherwise, all they do is put off the inevitable and spiral further into debt.

Assets may include cars, furniture, tools, toys, or simple garage sale items. They may also include jewelry, collectibles, coins, and investments.

We are also asked often about using savings or investments to pay off debts, such as including 401(k) or tax-deferred funds. We recommend this only as a last resort strategy. Once the money is gone, it's gone, and it's very difficult to accumulate again. There also may be withdrawal penalties and taxes due that make the cost of using this option very expensive. We encourage people to look to other solutions before selling investments or draining their savings.

PLUMB LINE PRINCIPLE

Turn my heart toward your statutes and not toward selfish gain.
—Psalm 119:36

Again, a key issue is working hard to solve the root causes for your current difficulty, not just putting out the small fires that started as a result of not examining the root causes. Selling assets and using debt sometimes only let us procrastinate in making the bigger, more difficult decisions.

Repairs: Your Credit Report

It is vitally important to check your credit report for any inaccuracies. Order a copy from one of the three major credit reporting agencies (Experian, TransUnion, and Equifax). Expect to pay a fee ranging from $8 to $12. When your credit report arrives, check it carefully. If you find an error, write a letter and send copies to the credit bureaus. The bureaus will check with the source of the information and send you an update. The dispute process can take up to thirty days. If you still disagree with the information, you can add your own statement to the credit report.

Financial software company Quicken recommends sending the following information when disputing items on your credit report:

- Your full name—first, middle, and last—and include any suffixes (Jr., Sr., II, etc.)
- Your complete mailing address
- Previous addresses for the past five years, including ZIP codes
- Your Social Security number (this is necessary to access your credit report)
- Your spouse's name and spouse's Social Security number (if applicable)
- Your date of birth

- The name and account number of the creditor and item in question
- The specific reason for your disagreement with the disputed item
- Your signature

Mail your dispute to the appropriate address listed in the appendix on page 224 of this book, or call these numbers for more information:

Experian 1-888-EXPERIAN
Equifax 1-800-378-2732
Trans Union 1-800-916-8800.

When the Pressure Is On

It's easy for people to become self-absorbed, especially when they're under pressure. We tend to focus on our own problems. This in turn can lead to seeing life through a distorted perspective.

PLUMB LINE PRINCIPLE
If anyone has this world's goods and sees his brother in need but shuts off his compassion from him—how can God's love reside in him?
—1 John 3:17 HCSB

If we are not serving others in some capacity, now may be the time to start. Every person should be involved in service, whether it is through a church, a volunteer organization, or another worthwhile entity. Often it's when we serve others that we see we're not the only ones who experience difficulties. We also have the satisfaction of helping others, without self-serving or hidden motives. We simply reach out and care.

Final Plumb Line Words of Encouragement

- Continually surrender control to God (stewardship vs. ownership).
- Study God's Word and His biblical, financial principles.
- Pray daily (with your spouse if you're married).

- Set your getaway retreat dates with your spouse (or decide how you will handle regular reviews of your budget).
- List (and assign) responsibilities and due dates.
- Write out your personal commitments and steps of action.
- Keep communication open and honest with your spouse or accountability partner.
- Press forward, living a disciplined life one day at a time.

PLUMB LINE PRINCIPLE
Therefore, whether we are at home or away, we make it our aim to be pleasing to Him.
—2 Corinthians 5:9 HCSB

We'd like to pray for you: *Father in heaven, we acknowledge our need for You and the reality that following You isn't always easy. However, we do want Your best for our lives. We want to be good stewards of the funds and resources You entrust to our care. May the person reading this prayer draw upon Your grace, through Your Holy Spirit, to move forward one day at a time. May we be found faithful in fulfilling our responsibilities while we trust You. May our lives, time, and the resources You entrust to us be a mighty tool in Your hand to reach others with Your love and grace, even to the very ends of the earth, so no one is lost without a saving knowledge of Jesus Christ. Amen.*

PLUMB LINE PRINCIPLE
Your righteousness reaches to the skies, O God, you who have done great things. Who, O God, is like you? Though you have made me see troubles, many and bitter, you will restore my life again; from the depths of the earth you will again bring me up. You will increase my honor and comfort me once again.
—Psalm 71:19–21

Application

What has God been talking to you about as you read this chapter?

What areas of your life do you still need to surrender to Jesus Christ and the working of the Holy Spirit?

What changes do you need to start incorporating in your life and finances?

What action steps will you take to get your financial house in order?

APPENDIXES

My/Our Personal Commitments

Date_____

Chapter 1—The Front Porch: Reflecting on the Past, Seeing a Vision for the Future

What do you want your financial house to look like?

What would you like to accomplish in your lifetime?

If you didn't have to earn any more money, what would you spend your time doing?

Chapter 2—Tools of the Trade: Safety Instructions and Leveling the Ground

Chapter 3—Foyer/Entryway: Stewardship
versus Ownership

Chapter 4—Laundry Room: Debt

Chapter 5—Master Bedroom: Husband and Wife
Financial Communication

Chapter 6—Dining Room: Charitable Giving,
Tithes, and Offerings

Chapter 7—Kitchen: A Recipe for Financial
Freedom (Planning and Budgeting)

Chapter 8—Children's Bedrooms: Children and
Money

Chapter 9—Den: Savings, Investing, Wills,
Retirement, and More

Chapter 10—Living Room: Making Your Plan
Work

Chapter 11—Guest Room: Single-Parent
Families

Chapter 12—Garage: Repairs and Maintenance

Other Notes

From Getting Your Financial House in Order *by David & Debbie Bragonier
with Kimn Gollnick (Broadman & Holman), copyright © 2003
Photocopying is permitted for personal use only.*

To-Do List

Date _____

God/Church
To Do   Target Date

1.

2.

3.

4.

5.

Family
To Do   Target Date

1.

2.

3.

4.

5.

Work
To Do   Target Date

1.

2.

3.

4.

5.

Finances
To Do   Target Date

1.

2.

3.

4.

5.

6.

7.

8.

9.

10.

Tasks
To Do   Target Date

1.

2.

3.

4.

5.

6.

7.

8.

9.

10.

11.

12.

13.

14.

15.

16.

17.

18.

19.

20.

Telephone Calls

Name/Message   Phone Number

1.

2.

3.

4.

5.

From Getting Your Financial House in Order *by David & Debbie Bragonier
with Kimn Gollnick (Broadman & Holman), copyright © 2003
Photocopying is permitted for personal use only.*

The Three Major Credit Bureaus

EQUIFAX	EXPERIAN	TRANS UNION, LLC
P. O. Box 740256	P. O. Box 919	P. O. Box 97328
Atlanta, GA 30374	Allen, TX 75013	Jackson, MS 39288
1-800-378-2732	1-888-EXPERIAN	1-800-916-8800

GOALS WORKSHEET

Date _____

One Year Goals

GOAL:

Action Steps   Target Date

1.

2.

3.

4.

5.

GOAL:

Action Steps   Target Date

1.

2.

3.

4.

5.

GOAL:

Action Steps   Target Date

1.

2.

3.

4.

5.

GOAL:

Action Steps   Target Date

1.

2.

3.

4.

5.

Five Year Goals

GOAL:

Action Steps   Target Date

1.

2.

3.

4.

5.

GOAL:

Action Steps   Target Date

1.

2.

3.

4.

5.

GOAL:

Action Steps   Target Date

1.

2.

3.

4.

5.

GOAL:

Action Steps   Target Date

1.

2.

3.

4.

5.

From Getting Your Financial House in Order *by David & Debbie Bragonier*
with Kimn Gollnick (Broadman & Holman), copyright © 2003
Photocopying is permitted for personal use only.

NOTES

Chapter 4: Laundry Room

1. Deborah Fowles, "The Epidemic of Affluenza," http://financialplan.about.com/library/weekly/aa060901a.htm, 28 September 2001.

2. "Personal Bankruptcies Continue Record-Setting Pace," Associated Press, *USA Today,* 15 May 2003, http://www.usa today.com/money/perfi/general/2003-05-15-bankrupt_x.htm, 22 May 2003.

3. "How to Get out of Debt," http://www.newyorklife. com/NYL2/PrintThis/1,1287,11195-13,00.html, 28 September 2001.

4. "Avoiding a House of (Credit) Cards," *Christian Science Monitor,* 6 August 2001.

5. Mike Coe, http://www.coeinc.org/AllSections/Debt.html, 6 May 2002.

6. Mark Cowan, "Higher Taxes Mean Less in Savings," in Family News in Focus, http://www.family.org/cforum/fnif/news/ a0017075.html, 3 August 2001.

7. Barna Research Online, http://wwwl.barna.org/cgi-bin/ PageCategory.asp?CategoryID=29, 19 April 2001.

Chapter 6: Dining Room

1. John and Sylvia Ronsvalle, "The State of Church Giving through 1999," www.emptytomb.org.

2. http://www.september11fund.org.

Chapter 7: Kitchen

1. Mike Coe, http://www.coeinc.org/financialstatistics.htm, 6 May 2002.

2. Ibid.

3. Gordon Botting, "Life after Debt," http://www.amazing-facts.org/ourministry/news/life_after_debt.html, 6 May 2002.

Chapter 8: Children's Bedrooms

1. Juliet B. Schor, *The Overspent American: Upscaling, Downshifting and the New Consumer* (Basic Books, 1998).

2. Libby Wells, "Card Issuers Target Teens for Latest Plastic Attacks," 8 May 2000, http://www.bankrate.com/brm/news/cc/20000508.asp, 26 July 2002.

3. Euna Kwon, Merrill Lynch, "Ten Ways to Talk with Your Teens about Money," http://www.christianwomentoday.com/money/tenteens.html, 25 March 2002.

Chapter 9: Den

1. Remarks by Sen. Larry E. Craig, 2002 National Summit on Retirement Savings, http://www.saversummit.dol.gov/craig.html, 27 February 2002.

2. Mark Cowan, "Higher Taxes Mean Less in Savings," in Family News in Focus, http://www.family.org/cforum/fnif/news/a0017075.html, 3 August 2001.

3. "Teach Your Children the Value of Money," http://fc.standardandpoors.com/srl/wac/library_article.jsp?tid=0082, 26 August 2002.

4. American Savings education Council, "Top 10 Ways to Beat the Clock and Save for Retirement," http://www.asec.org/topten.html, 11 May 2002.

5. Eileen Alt Powell, "Confidence, Savings Rate Don't Match," 27 February 2002, http://www.ncpa.org/iss/eco/2002/pd022802c.html, 11 May 2002.

6. Julie Sturgeon, "Just the Facts on Life Insurance," http://www.bankrate.com/brm/news/insur/20020201a.asp?keyword=CDSAVINGS, 1 February 2002.

7. "Life Advice about Making a Will," http://www.rfsco.com/gt/issues/2000/dec2000/1.html, 11 May 2002.

Chapter 11: Guest Room

1. Coe, http://www.coeinc.org/financialstatistics.htm, 6 May 2002.

2. March 2000 Federal Census, http://www.census.gov/Press-Release/www/2001/cb01-113.html, 28 July 2002.